The Possibility of Culture

New Directions in Aesthetics

Series editors: Dominic McIver Lopes, University of British Columbia, and Berys Gaut, University of St Andrews

Blackwell's New Directions in Aesthetics series highlights ambitious single- and multiple-author books that confront the most intriguing and pressing problems in aesthetics and the philosophy of art today. Each book is written in a way that advances understanding of the subject at hand and is accessible to upper-undergraduate and graduate students.

1. *Interpretation and Construction: Art, Speech, and the Law*
   by Robert Stecker
2. *Art as Performance*
   by David Davies
3. *The Performance of Reading: An Essay in the Philosophy of Literature*
   by Peter Kivy
4. *The Art of Theater*
   by James R. Hamilton
5. *Cultural Appropriation and the Arts*
   by James O. Young
6. *Photography and Philosophy: Essays on the Pencil of Nature*
   ed. Scott Walden
7. *Art and Ethical Criticism*
   ed. Garry L. Hagberg
8. *Mirrors to One Another: Emotion and Value in Jane Austen and David Hume*
   by Eva Dadlez
9. *Comic Relief: A Comprehensive Philosophy of Humor*
   by John Morreall
10. *The Art of Videogames*
    by Grant Tavinor
11. *Once-Told Tales: An Essay in Literary Aesthetics*
    by Peter Kivy
12. *The Art of Comics: A Philosophical Approach*
    by Aaron Meskin and Roy T. Cook
13. *The Aesthetics of Wine*
    by Douglas Burnham and Ole Martin Skilleås
14. *The Possibility of Culture: Pleasure and Moral Development in Kant's Aesthetics*
    by Bradley Murray

The Possibility of Culture

*Pleasure and Moral Development
in Kant's Aesthetics*

BRADLEY MURRAY

This edition first published 2015
© 2015 John Wiley & Sons, Inc.

Registered Office
John Wiley & Sons, Ltd, The Atrium, Southern Gate, Chichester, West Sussex,
PO19 8SQ, UK

Editorial Offices
350 Main Street, Malden, MA 02148-5020, USA
9600 Garsington Road, Oxford, OX4 2DQ, UK
The Atrium, Southern Gate, Chichester, West Sussex, PO19 8SQ, UK

For details of our global editorial offices, for customer services, and for information about
how to apply for permission to reuse the copyright material in this book please see our
website at www.wiley.com/wiley-blackwell.

The right of Bradley Murray to be identified as the author of this work has been asserted in
accordance with the UK Copyright, Designs and Patents Act 1988.

Library of Congress Cataloging-in-Publication Data
Murray, Bradley, 1980–
  The possibility of culture : pleasure and moral development in Kant's aesthetics /
Bradley Murray.
      pages   cm
  Includes bibliographical references and index.
  ISBN 978-1-118-95065-4 (cloth)
1. Kant, Immanuel, 1724–1804.   2. Aesthetics.   3. Ethics.   I. Title.
  B2799.A4M87 2015
  111'.85092–dc23

                                                        2015000032
A catalogue record for this book is available from the British Library.

Cover image: The Apotheosis of Homer, 1827, by Jean Auguste Dominique Ingres.
© DeAgostini/Superstock

Set in 10.5/13.5pt Galliard by SPi Global, Pondicherry, India
Printed and bound in Malaysia by Vivar Printing Sdn Bhd

1   2015

To my parents, Diane Murray and Eric Murray

Contents

Acknowledgements   viii
Note on Citations   ix

Introduction   1

1   Aesthetics and Culture in Context   13

2   Beauty and Love   31

3   Beauty and Disinterestedness   46

4   Art, Genius, and Abstraction   66

5   Sublimity and Esteem   84

6   Choosing Culture Over Happiness   105

7   Conclusion   122

Bibliography   138
Index   143

Acknowledgements

I was very fortunate to have had the opportunity to present early versions of the chapters of this book to the Aesthetics Reading Group at the University of British Columbia. I received many insightful comments which led me to rethink a number of my ideas about Kant's aesthetics. I have also benefited from the feedback that I received from three anonymous reviewers commissioned by Wiley-Blackwell. I have done my best to address the points raised by all who have read the manuscript closely, and I hope that they will find my attempts at improving it to be at least somewhat satisfying. I would especially like to thank Dominic McIver Lopes for the many challenging and helpful ideas with which he presented me as this project was taking shape.

Note on Citations

Citations of Kant's texts indicate an abbreviated title, along with the volume and page number of the Academy edition of Kant's writings (*Kant's Gesammelte Schriften*, Akademie Ausgabe [Berlin: de Gruyter, 1900–]). Unless otherwise noted, translations are from the *Cambridge Edition of the Works of Immanuel Kant* (Cambridge: Cambridge University Press, 1992–) (Ca).

Anthropology	(1798) Anthropology from a Pragmatic Point of View, Ca Anthropology, History, and Education
CJ	(1790) Critique of Judgment, *Critique of Judgement*, trans. J. C. Meredith (Oxford: Oxford University Press)
Concept of Race	(1785) Determination of the Concept of a Human Race, Ca Anthropology, History, and Education
Conflict	(1798) The Conflict of the Faculties, Ca Religion and Rational Theology
CPR	(1781) Critique of Pure Reason, Ca Critique of Pure Reason
CPrR	(1788) Critique of Practical Reason, Ca Practical Philosophy
Enlightenment	(1784) An Answer to the Question: What is Enlightenment?, Ca Practical Philosophy
Ethics	Lectures on Ethics, Ca Lectures on Ethics

FI   First Introduction to the Critique of Judgment, Ca Critique of the Power of Judgment

Groundwork   (1785) Groundwork of the Metaphysics of Morals, Ca Practical Philosophy

Idea   (1784) Idea for a Universal History with a Cosmopolitan Aim, Ca Anthropology, History, and Education

Lectures on Anthropology   Lectures on Anthropology, Ca Lectures on Anthropology

Magnitudes   (1763) Attempt to Introduce the Concept of Negative Magnitudes into Philosophy, Ca Theoretical Philosophy

Maladies   (1764) Essay on the Maladies of the Head, Ca Anthropology, History, and Education

Metaphysics   Lectures on Metaphysics, Ca Lectures on Metaphysics

Morals   (1797) The Metaphysics of Morals, Ca Practical Philosophy

Observations   (1764) Observations on the Beautiful and the Sublime, Ca Anthropology, History, and Education

Peace   (1795) Toward Perpetual Peace, Ca Practical Philosophy

Pedagogy   (1803) Lectures on Pedagogy, Ca Anthropology, History, and Education

Religion   (1793) Religion Within the Boundaries of Mere Reason, Ca Religion and Rational Theology

Theory   (1793) On the Common Saying: That May be True in Theory, But It is of No Use in Practice, Ca Practical Philosophy

Introduction

In his *Discourse on the Sciences and Arts*, Rousseau claimed that princes who are out to keep the people in chains encourage them to acquire a taste for the arts.[1] Those placated by beauty, in other words, will be too caught up in their personal pleasure to raise troublesome questions about the social order. It is no longer 1750, but we still find ourselves confronted in certain ways by Rousseau's provocation. How can we justify devoting time and resources to beauty when the societies in which we live face so many substantial problems? "Islands of beauty" certainly offer temporary relief in a troubling world; but, surely, there is no virtue in choosing to seek shelter on an albeit pleasure-filled aesthetic island instead of devoting our time to trying to improve the world directly – through genuine commitment, sacrifice, and confrontation of the powers that be.[2]

This anti-aesthetic line of thought is relevant to artists, who must decide whether to create artworks aiming to enable audiences to enjoy experiences of beauty, or to create other sorts of works – such as those designed to be challenging politically. It is also relevant to artists' audiences, who must decide whether to spend time engaging with works that will offer them the pleasure of beauty, rather than engaging with works that are not designed to please in this way. For that matter, both

The Possibility of Culture: Pleasure and Moral Development in Kant's Aesthetics,
First Edition. Bradley Murray.
© 2015 John Wiley & Sons, Inc. Published 2015 by John Wiley & Sons, Inc.

artists and audiences face a decision as to whether they might be better off devoting their time to entirely non-artistic pursuits that might do something directly to improve the world's problems. And, of course, this anti-aesthetic line of thought applies not just to the pursuit of artistic beauty, but also to that of natural beauty. Should the nature lover allow himself or herself the pleasure of more-or-less purposeless nature walks – with no purpose, that is, other than the appreciation of landscapes, flowers, and other such things? Or might this individual do better to spend time on more practical activities that might more directly play a part in improving the world?

The present study addresses Kant's aesthetics with the aim of bringing out the ethical priorities that underlie its account of aesthetic pleasure. We will see that Kant's account constitutes a compelling challenge to the sort of anti-aesthetic thought just mentioned. It will emerge that, unlike some thinkers with whom he engages – and most notably Rousseau – Kant holds that there can be no ethical objection to pursuing either beauty or the other aesthetic pleasure that he takes up, the pleasure of sublimity. Instead, he holds that by pursuing aesthetic pleasure, we put ourselves in a position to develop morally as individuals by becoming better able to put aside our personal inclinations when needed. Moral development at the individual level, in turn, makes possible social progress, more generally. Another way to put the same point is to say that, on Kant's view, the *culture of the individual* occurs in a way that is closely connected with the *culture of humanity* as a whole.

We will focus in the chapters that follow on the contribution of aesthetic pleasure to the culture of the individual. But it is worth considering at the outset Kant's broader vision of the culture of humanity as a whole, which he understands to be a process that ideally culminates in morally sophisticated forms of social organization. In *On the Common Saying: That May be True in Theory, But It is of No Use in Practice*, Kant specifies that a morally developed society will be one which is grounded in "[t]he *freedom* of every member of the society as a human being," his or her "*equality* with every other as a *subject*," and "[t]he *independence* of every member of a commonwealth as a citizen." The freedom that Kant envisions partly includes the freedom to pursue one's own conception of happiness. As Kant puts it, "[n]o one can coerce me to be happy in his way," and "each may seek his happiness in the way that seems good to him, provided he does not infringe upon that freedom of others to strive for a like end which can coexist with the freedom of everyone in accordance with a possible universal law (i.e., does not infringe upon this right of another)."[3] In such a society, Kant claims, individuals will also be free when it comes to the "public use of reason." This amounts to a kind of freedom of speech primarily relating to the debate of ideas. Using reason publicly involves considering oneself "as a member of a whole commonwealth, even of the society of citizens of the world," and making use of one's reason "*as a scholar* before the entire public of the *world of readers*."[4] In exercising reason publicly, we do not limit our thinking to prevailing norms associated with the current social order, but allow ourselves to entertain ideas that call into question that very social order. The development of our capacities to exercise our reason publicly amounts to our enlightenment, or our emergence from a "self-incurred minority" in which we lack the courage to reason "without direction from another." Hence, the motto of enlightenment: "*Sapere aude!* Have courage to make use of your *own* understanding!"[5]

While Kant advocates for social change in the form of increased freedom, equality, and independence, his view is that this must occur through gradual developmental processes. He is, therefore, generally opposed to revolutionary change.[6] Kant holds that individual moral development contributes to the gradual development of society, since morally sophisticated individuals – both leaders and citizens – are less likely to face moral impediments from their inclinations. Leaders in positions of power who lack moral sophistication will tend to act primarily on the basis of principles of self-love, pursuing their inclinations at the expense of the well-being of citizens. Citizens who lack moral sophistication might be too consumed with their personal inclinations to recognize infringements on the rights of fellow citizens; or, if they do recognize these, may lack the capacity to abandon their self-concern in order to take action to bring about a more just state of affairs.[7]

We find in Kant's account of development at the level of the individual, and of society as a whole, a certain amount of hope that things can and will improve. Still, Kant does not maintain a Pollyannaish conception of human nature. In the *Idea for a Universal History with a Cosmopolitan Aim*, he seeks to explain the development of society partly in terms of the tensions inherent in social organization itself. There is, he asserts, a fundamental antagonism between the individual and society given that human beings manifest what he calls "unsociable sociability." As human beings, we have a propensity to enter into society, yet we also exhibit "a thoroughgoing resistance that constantly threatens to break up this society."[8] The task we face, Kant asserts, is to implement a form of civil society that nurtures our unsociable sociability. Such a society is one that enables freedom by enabling "a thoroughgoing antagonism of its members," while at the same time imposing a form of order which gives rise to "the most precise determination and security of the boundaries of this freedom."[9]

To return to the anti-aesthetic line of thought mentioned a moment ago, the Kantian reply will be that the pursuit of beauty facilitates individual moral development, which, in turn, contributes to social progress. Thus, in seeking out experiences of beauty, we do not isolate ourselves on an "island of relief," but put ourselves in a position to respond more helpfully to the world around us. As we will see more clearly in the chapters that follow, the contribution of aesthetic pleasure lies in its capacity to teach us to step back from our ordinary tendencies to act self-interestedly in the pursuit of our inclinations.[10]

Talk of Kant's views on social progress forces us to face up to an unfortunate irony. Kant holds some very racist views, underpinned by a view of white Europeans as positioned at the pinnacle of a hierarchy of races. In Kant's eyes, whites occupy this position partly because of their capacity to be civilized and to engage in precisely the process of culture at the individual and social levels just mentioned. In the *Lectures on Anthropology*, for instance, he maintains that white Europeans "are always making progress" when it comes to the "perfection of human nature."[11] While we might like to avoid recalling Kant's views on race, it is not possible to do so in the context of a discussion of his conception of culture. If Kant's theory actually entails such racism, then contemporary readers can hardly use it as a guide in thinking about how the pursuit of aesthetic pleasure might contribute to social progress – which we take to include the eradication of forms of mistreatment, including racial discrimination. In fact, we have reason to think that there is no necessary connection between Kant's views on race and his aesthetic theory. Instead, these seem to be his personal views, and he seems to have derived them partly from empirical theories of race that were prevalent at the time he lived. If the crucial claim for present purposes is that the pursuit of aesthetic pleasure can help us to develop skill in distancing ourselves from our inclinations, there is absolutely no good reason for

Kant or anyone else to suggest that the capacity to develop such a skill is tied to race. This would be a false empirical claim, and it is properly dropped from a plausible reconstruction of Kant's aesthetic theory. Of course, the fact that we need to drop this claim – and perhaps other even less controversial empirical or philosophical claims – in reconstructing Kant's theory does not speak against engaging with his theory to begin with. Kant was an eighteenth-century European thinker with a view of the world that needs updating, but this does not entail that his work should be wholly rejected.

In fact, when we delve more deeply into Kant's views, we find that his views on race interact in complicated ways with his moral and political philosophy. On the one hand, we have just seen, he accepts that people have different capacities for culture depending on the racial group to which they belong. But on the other hand, he is wedded to the core principles of his moral and political theories, including the principle that every human being – regardless of race – is to be treated equally, guaranteed freedom, and never used merely as means to another human being's end.[12] Because he holds such views, Kant does not ultimately seem to believe that the racial hierarchy that he accepts has very many implications when it comes to the question of how members of particular racial groups are to be treated. To this end, he comes out against slavery and colonialism, particularly in his later writings. In the *Metaphysics of Morals*, for example, he considers whether it can be acceptable for a nation to settle on the land of a people who are "shepherds or hunters (like the Hottentots, the Tungusi, or most of the American Indian nations) who depend for their sustenance on great open regions."[13] Kant's view is that such settlement is only acceptable when it takes place in a way that involves a fair contract. This is true, he continues, "despite the fact that sufficient specious reasons to justify the use of force are available; that it is to the world's advantage, partly because these crude peoples will become civilized."[14] Kant is not persuaded by the argument that many of his contemporaries would have accepted, namely that colonial expansion through force is justified on the grounds of civilizing a "crude" people. As he puts it in *Toward Perpetual Peace*, published in 1795, "the *inhospitable* behaviour of civilized, especially commercial, states in our part of the world, the injustice they show in *visiting* foreign lands and peoples (which with them is tantamount to *conquering* them) goes to horrifying lengths."[15]

A knee-jerk response, which some new to Kant find themselves having, would be to classify him as an outdated thinker, and to refuse to engage with his work – including his work in aesthetic theory. However, such a response is ultimately not sustainable. Kant's influence is lasting, and makes itself apparent in the often subtle ways in which his ideas shape the agendas of current debates among those working in aesthetics and the philosophy of art, art criticism, and art theory. Not only do those who agree with his views attend to them. Those who could not disagree more fundamentally with Kant also find themselves compelled to engage, at least to some extent, with his views. It makes sense for us to continue to return to Kant's aesthetics. This is especially true today, at a time when philosophers of art are vigorously pursuing questions concerning the interaction of art and morality,[16] and when these philosophers, as well as art critics, are beginning to question a decades-long rejection of beauty that has been motivated at least partly by the kinds of ethical considerations mentioned at the outset.[17]

Since the issues in Kant's aesthetics that we will pursue are relevant quite widely, I have attempted to present the material in a way that might appeal not just to Kant scholars, but also to more general readers. This has partly involved avoiding lengthy discussions of the various interpretations of Kant's views that have emerged over the years. Instead, where I have deemed it helpful, I have included notes referring the reader to relevant secondary literature.

Although this book addresses many of the topics that are covered in standard approaches to Kant's aesthetics, the present approach is "non-standard" in a couple of ways. The first, of course, is that its emphasis is on the ethical priorities that underlie Kant's account of aesthetic pleasure. Consequently, relatively little emphasis is placed on Kant's attempted solution to the problem of justifying aesthetic judgments. This is a problem that Kant had inherited in large part from Hume. In his essay "Of the Standard of Taste," Hume addressed a problem that seems to arise when we assume that judgments of taste are based on subjective experiences of pleasure and that the quality of beauty is not strictly speaking a quality of objects.[18] Given the subjectivity of taste, it is not immediately obvious why we might be entitled to believe that there could be anything approaching a standard of taste. Yet we apparently are deeply committed to the view that there is a standard of taste, and the problem is to find a way of articulating how such a standard is possible. Kant, like Hume, starts from the assumption that beauty is a subjective experience of pleasure, and he also accepts that beauty is not a quality in objects. As Kant puts it, beauty – and in fact any feeling of pleasure and displeasure – "denotes nothing in the object, but is a feeling which the subject has of itself and of the manner in which it is affected by the representation."[19]

Although Kant shares Hume's concern with the general issue of aesthetic justification, he approaches the issue differently. For Kant, the priority is not to articulate a standard of taste, *per se*, but rather to focus in detail on the underlying logical form of judgments of taste, and to seek an answer to the question of what could justify judgments with just such a form. He takes up the task of analyzing the logical form of aesthetic judgments in the "Analytic of the Beautiful" of the Critique of Aesthetic Judgment. Having analyzed their form, he then attempts to provide a "deduction" of such judgments, which aims to establish their validity. Other than briefly reviewing Kant's approach to the issue of justification as part of an overall assessment of the present interpretation in the book's conclusion, engaging with the details of this approach will not be a priority.[20]

The second way in which the present approach to Kant's aesthetics is non-standard is that it looks beyond the most widely known text in Kantian aesthetics – namely, the *Critique of Judgment*. It would be difficult if not impossible to understand how Kant's ethical views influence his views on the legitimacy of the pursuit of the pleasure of beauty if we did not do this. Although these views are sometimes vaguely alluded to in the account that we find in the third *Critique*, Kant does not always make fully explicit the relevant connections. Among the most important of Kant's other texts are the *Metaphysics of Morals* and *Anthropology from a Pragmatic Point of View*. These represent a side of Kant's ethical thought that is far less dogmatic, and in many ways more willing to engage realistically with our limitations as human beings, than the side that emerges in simple caricatures of his moral philosophy. The reconstruction of Kant's views on the ethical implications of the pursuit of aesthetic pleasure that we will pursue will depend heavily on the anthropological and moral psychological views that he develops in works such as these.

Here is a brief overview of the chapters that follow. Chapter 1 explores Kant's two principal reasons for pursuing connections between aesthetic pleasure and moral development. The first is that he wishes to engage with Rousseau's anti-aesthetic views; the second is that he is interested in developing a theory of culture, a task which partly involves specifying means by which we may pursue culture. Pursuing aesthetic pleasure will turn out to be one means by which we may do this. After outlining the stages of culture that Kant envisions, the chapter concludes by exploring the interaction between his moral theory – in which the notion of dutiful action plays a central role – and his conception of culture.

One way in which Kant takes the pleasure of beauty to contribute to moral development is by means of the former's connection with the emotion of love, and the aim of Chapter 2 is to explore and develop this picture. It is suggested that a satisfying reconstruction of Kant's view will be one that invokes a crucial feature of his account of the pleasure of beauty, namely its connection with what he calls "subjective finality." Along these lines, a reconstruction is pursued according to which the pleasure of beauty, because it is bound up with subjective finality, is closely connected with gratitude, which, in turn, can contribute to our capacity to feel a morally relevant feeling of love.

Chapter 3 seeks to understand the moral implications of the Kantian view that the pleasure of beauty is characterized by disinterestedness. Starting with the assumption that this conception of aesthetic pleasure is, generally speaking, a plausible one, the chapter examines Kant's account of the connections between disinterestedness and existence, and between disinterestedness and understanding. It then explores Kant's reasons for thinking that the pleasure of beauty can contribute to our moral development in virtue of its disinterestedness.

The aim of Chapter 4 is to consider whether it is less effective, as some might think, to pursue culture through engagement with the arts than with nature. After considering Kant's response to the Rousseauian suggestion that the pursuit of the arts is bound up with problematic attitudes and emotions, the chapter explores Kant's suggestion that it is necessary to carry out an act of "abstraction" to experience the beauty of certain objects, including artifacts. An "epistemological" interpretation is offered of his account of artistic genius according to which it functions as an extension of his account of abstraction.

Chapter 5 shifts the focus from the pleasure of beauty to the pleasure of sublimity, in order to consider how the latter, like the former, might contribute to our moral development. The chapter centers around Kant's suggestion that this development might occur owing to the fact that the pleasure of sublimity is connected with the feeling of respect or esteem (just as the pleasure of beauty is connected with the feeling of love). Although, it is argued, there are ultimately difficulties with such an account, the chapter concludes by suggesting that there remains a place for sublimity in Kant's account of culture.

Whereas many of Kant's principal opponents have needed no convincing of the claim that it is important to pursue culture – they simply disagree over whether the pursuit of aesthetic pleasure is a way to do it – there will be others who do not see why it is worth devoting attention to culture, in the first place. Chapter 6 pursues Kant's argument for the claim that we have reason to pursue culture, and, specifically, to do so when faced with a choice between pursuing culture or pursuing happiness. The chapter begins by briefly considering Kant's attempts at arguing for this conclusion in the *Metaphysics of Morals* and *Groundwork of the Metaphysics of Morals*, before focusing on his argument in the Appendix to the Critique of Teleological Judgment.

The book concludes by briefly addressing two general issues raised by the discussion of the preceding chapters. The first is the issue of what, if any, moral significance the experience of ugliness might have. The next issue has to do with the place of empirical claims in Kantian aesthetics. The development of Kant's aesthetic theory pursued here rests on empirical claims, including claims that can be seen to derive from what Kant calls "pragmatic anthropology." Assuming that there is a place for empirical claims in a philosophical theory, generally speaking, the question remains as to whether this is compatible with Kant's vision of philosophy. If it were not, this might be considered to be a reason for adopting a more "standard" approach to Kant's aesthetics focusing on his examination of the issue of aesthetic justification. After outlining this standard approach, it is suggested that even on such an approach, Kantian aesthetics seems ultimately grounded in core empirical claims – a fact which should lead us to be open to the present approach.

Notes

1 Jean-Jacques Rousseau, *"The Discourses" and Other Early Political Writings*, ed. Victor Gourevitch (Cambridge: Cambridge University Press, 1997), 7n.
2 See Arthur Danto, *The Abuse of Beauty: Aesthetics and the Concept of Art* (Chicago: Open Court, 2003), 116.

3   Theory 8:290.

4   Enlightenment 8:37. See also Howard L. Williams, *Kant's Political Philosophy* (Oxford: Basil Blackwell, 1986), 154.

5   Enlightenment 8:35.

6   In the *Metaphysics of Morals*, for instance, Kant writes that there is "no right to sedition (*seditio*), still less to rebellion (*rebellio*), and least of all is there a right against the head of a state as an individual person (the monarch), to attack his person or even his life (*monarcho-machismus sub specie tyrannicidii*) on the pretext that he has abused his authority (*tyrannis*)" (Morals 6:320).

7   There is, in fact, a reciprocal relationship between the culture of the individual and the culture of humanity, according to Kant. He holds not just that individual moral development contributes to the development of society as a whole, but also that the development of human society contributes to individual moral development. Living in society helps us to develop rationally, and this rational development, in turn, serves to enable individuals to choose to act in ways that are not merely based on principles of self-love. The importance of human society in this account lies in the fact that society can be expected to outlive any particular human being, and rational gains occur over the course of human history. Thus, in the *Idea for a Universal History*, Kant asserts that predispositions toward rationality can "develop completely only in the species, but not in the individual," and this is because it is beyond the capacity of any individual fully to make use of his or her natural predisposition toward reason (Idea 8:18). Any individual "would have to live exceedingly long" in order to be able fully to develop as a rational agent. Rationality develops over a series of generations, "each of which transmits its enlightenment to the next" (Idea 8:19).

8   Idea 8:20.

9   Idea 8:22. See Allen Wood, "Kant's Fourth Proposition: The Unsociable Sociability of Human Nature," in *Kant's Idea for a Universal History with a Cosmopolitan Aim*, ed. Amélie Oksenberg Rorty and James Schmidt (Cambridge: Cambridge University Press, 2009).

10   Kant, of course, is by no means alone in suggesting that experiencing aesthetic pleasure can help us to gain this kind of perspective. For example, Iris Murdoch has suggested that beauty helps us to cultivate the capacity to engage in "unselfing," and by this she has in mind something at least somewhat related to Kant's view (*The Sovereignty of Good* [London: Ark Paperbacks, Routledge & Kegan Paul, 1985], 85). And Herbert Marcuse points out that although progressive social movements have tended to be suspicious of beauty, they have normally come to see its value in the end. On the one hand, he suggests, there has been a tendency to reject beauty

as a category of "bourgeois" aesthetics. But on the other hand, "the idea of Beauty appears time and again in progressive movements, as an aspect of the reconstruction of nature and society." From Marcuse's perspective, the potential of beauty lies partly in its capacity to challenge "the prevailing reality principle of domination" (*The Aesthetic Dimension* [Boston: Beacon Press, 1979], 63).

11 Lectures on Anthropology 25:840. The classificatory scheme that Kant adopts involves a division of the human species into four different races: "the *whites, the yellow* Indians, the *Negroes*, and the *copper-red* Americans" (Concept of Race 8:93). Comparing black people with native Americans, he writes that "Americans have such relations in their nature that they will not become more perfect," whereas "[t]he Negroes are also not susceptible of further civilization, but they have instinct and discipline, which the Americans lack" (Lectures on Anthropology 25:843). Kant compares both groups to "[t]he Indians and Chinese," who, according to him, "appear to be at a standstill in their perfection; for their history books show that they now know no more than they have for a long time" (Lectures on Anthropology 25:843). Beyond this, Kant writes that "[Native Americans] are deficient in feeling (affects and passions), and resist civilization. [Africans, by contrast] are excessive in feelings; they have a strong sense of honor, and can be educated, but chiefly for servitude." Asians are "educable in the highest degree, but only for arts and not for sciences; they do not advance culture" (Lectures on Anthropology 25:1187). See also the *Observations on the Beautiful and the Sublime*, where Kant takes up Hume's views on black people: "Mr. Hume challenges anyone to adduce a single example where a Negro has demonstrated talents, and asserts that among the hundreds of thousands of blacks who have been transported elsewhere from their countries, although very many of them have been set free, nevertheless not a single one has ever been found who has accomplished something great in art or science or shown any other praiseworthy quality, while among the whites there are always those who rise up from the lowest rabble and through extraordinary gifts earn respect in the world" (Observations 2:253).

12 There is, however, some controversy over whether Kant's empirical views on race interfere with claims to universality that he wishes to build into his moral theory. For more on the interaction between Kant's views on race and his moral philosophy, see Robert B. Louden, *Kant's Impure Ethics: From Rational Beings to Human Beings* (Oxford: Oxford University Press, 2002); Pauline Kleingeld, "Kant's Second Thoughts on Race," *The Philosophical Quarterly* 57, no. 229 (2007): 573–592; and Emmanuel Chukwudi Eze, "The Color of Reason: The Idea of 'Race' in Kant's Anthropology," in *Postcolonial African Philosophy: A Reader*, ed. E. Chukwudi (Oxford: Blackwell, 1997), 103–140.

13   Morals 6:352.

14   Morals 6:352.

15   Peace 8:358.

16   See for example Berys Gaut, *Art, Emotion and Ethics* (Oxford: Oxford University Press, 2009); Jerrold Levinson, *Aesthetics and Ethics* (Cambridge: Cambridge University Press, 2001); and Noel Carroll, "Art and Ethical Criticism: An Overview of Recent Directions of Research," *Ethics* 110, no. 2 (January 2000): 350–387. The themes that will be taken up here concern what Gaut refers to as the "causal question," or the question of whether exposure to works of art tends to affect us morally, and if so whether it tends morally to improve or to corrupt us (*Art, Emotion and Ethics*, 6).

17   For example, see Alexander Nehamas, *Only a Promise of Happiness: The Place of Beauty in a World of Art* (Princeton: Princeton University Press, 2010); Danto, *Abuse of Beauty*; Wendy Steiner, *Venus in Exile* (New York: The Free Press, 2001); and Dave Hickey, *The Invisible Dragon: Four Essays on Beauty* (Los Angeles: Art Issues Press/Foundation for Advanced Critical Studies, 1993).

18   David Hume, "Of the Standard of Taste," in *Essays, Moral, Political, and Literary* (Indianapolis: Liberty Classics, 1987), 231–258.

19   CJ 5:203–204.

20   Books that focus more directly on the issue of aesthetic justification include Paul Guyer, *Kant and the Claims of Taste* (Cambridge: Cambridge University Press, 1997); Henry Allison, *Kant's Theory of Taste: A Reading of the Critique of Aesthetic Judgment* (Cambridge: Cambridge University Press, 2001); and Donald Crawford, *Kant's Aesthetic Theory* (Madison: University of Wisconsin Press, 1974).

1

Aesthetics and Culture in Context

A Pettiness of Soul

Kantian aesthetics provides a framework within which to conceptualize various connections between the pursuit of aesthetic pleasure and culture. But Kant does not always make these connections fully explicit in his principal writings, including his writings in aesthetics. In the present chapter, we will take a first step toward understanding Kant's view by considering two of his underlying reasons for attempting to articulate such connections in the first place. The first is that he wishes to engage with the kind of anti-aesthetic thought, based in large part on ethical considerations, that Rousseau advanced. The second reason is that he accepts the general view that we may pursue a developmental process through which we can become more sophisticated moral agents – the process of culture – and he wishes to understand how the pursuit of aesthetic pleasure might be a means by which we can pursue this process. In what follows, we will examine, in turn, each of these reasons.

Rousseau's anti-aestheticism, to begin with, is grounded partly in his concern that a society in which the taste for luxury is widespread – including the supposed luxury of artistic beauty – will be less free, and its members will be less virtuous. Princes, he claims, "always view with

The Possibility of Culture: Pleasure and Moral Development in Kant's Aesthetics,
First Edition. Bradley Murray.
© 2015 John Wiley & Sons, Inc. Published 2015 by John Wiley & Sons, Inc.

pleasure the dissemination among their subjects of a taste for the agreeable Arts and for superfluities which entail no export of monies," since "besides thus nurturing in them that pettiness of soul so suited to servitude, they well know that all the needs which a People imposes on itself are so many chains which it assumes."[1] Kant, in his 1784/5 ethics lectures, points out that the issue of luxury "has long been an object of philosophic consideration," and that philosophers have been particularly concerned to know "whether it ought to be approved or disapproved, and whether it conforms to morality or is opposed to it."[2] He addresses Rousseau's position directly, tracing it back to what he calls the "Cynic ideal," whose ancient defender was Diogenes. Kant, in fact, refers to Rousseau as "that subtle Diogenes" of modern times.[3]

In the ethics lectures, Kant approaches the issue of luxury partly from the point of view of individual happiness. Diogenes' view, Kant claims, is that "the means of happiness [are] negative" as "man is by nature content with little."[4] Kant agrees that the pursuit of luxury risks leading us away from happiness. In fact, he takes seriously the possibility that becoming overly caught up in the pursuit of luxury can make us suicidal. It makes us dependent on things which we may one day no longer be able to procure for ourselves. When we cannot enjoy a luxury on which we have come to depend, he claims, we may then be "thrown into all kinds of distress, so that we may even proceed to do away with ourselves."[5]

In addition to claiming that the pursuit of luxury risks contributing to our unhappiness, Kant also maintains that its pursuit can serve as a hindrance to us as moral agents. The trouble, he claims, is that insofar as getting caught up in the pursuit of luxury "multiplies our needs," it also "increases the enticements and attractions of inclination." Since our inclinations can lead us away from acting in conformity with our moral duties, anything that might increase our dependence on the inclinations is potentially dangerous from a moral point of view. As Kant puts it, when we depend too heavily on luxury, "it becomes hard to comply with morality; for the simpler and more innocent our needs, the less we are liable to err in fulfilling them." Thus, the pursuit of luxury may indirectly constitute "an incursion upon morality."[6]

In spite of his reservations concerning the pursuit of luxury, Kant does not advocate avoiding it altogether. Rather, he maintains that if we are going to pursue luxury, we should exercise moderation in doing so.

Thus, he claims, "there can be no objection to luxury from the moral point of view, save only that there must be laws, not to restrict it, but to furnish guidance,"[7] and as long as an individual violates neither duties to himself, nor duties to others in pursuing luxury, he "may enjoy as much pleasure as he has the ability and taste for."[8] In fact, not only does Kant see no objection to pursuing luxury in appropriate ways, he also maintains that there is a sense in which pursuing luxury can be advantageous to us insofar as we wish to develop morally. He holds this view because he thinks of luxuries as potentially amounting to helpful "diversions." His thought is that if we have a choice between pursuing a luxurious pleasure – which he takes to be a refined pleasure – and a pleasure merely tied to our immediate sensory gratification, it is better to pursue the luxurious one. Thus, in the *Anthropology*, Kant suggests that the pursuit of the arts, specifically, can serve as a helpful diversion, since when one "entertains himself with fine arts instead of mere sensual pleasures, he has the added satisfaction that he (as a refined man) is capable of such pleasures," and his pleasure will amount to enjoyment "in such objects that it does us credit to be occupied with."[9]

Thus, Kant and Rousseau are agreed that the arts are luxuries, and that luxuries are diversions. But they disagree over whether the diversion is helpful in the long run, especially when it comes to culture. Moreover, because Kant holds that luxury, as diversion, can help us to develop morally as individuals, and because, as we have seen, he holds that moral development at the individual level makes possible social progress, he is in a position to hold that pursuing the luxury of the arts can contribute, indirectly, to the improvement of society.

Although Kant, unlike Rousseau, supports the pursuit of the arts – even insofar as this amounts to the pursuit of a luxurious pleasure – he does not think that the pursuit of just any pleasure serves to promote our moral development. The pursuit of the pleasure of "agreeableness" is Kant's prime example of an unhelpful pleasure. Kant takes the pleasure of agreeableness to be "a delight pathologically conditioned (by stimuli)."[10] Sweets or wine can please our senses in a very immediate way, if we are fond of them, yet the pleasure has an addictive and self-centered quality. The object is considered insofar as it is capable of continuing to please *me*. As Kant puts it, the pleasure presupposes "the bearing [the object's] existence has upon my state so far as it is affected by such an object."[11] It is in this way that the pleasure of agreeableness is bound up with a "represented bond of connection between the Subject and the real existence of the object."[12] In other words, the pleasure is bound up with a representation of the object's continuing to exist. As part of this representation, *I*, the subject, continue in the future to stand in a relation to the object – namely, the relation of being pleased by it.

In experiencing the pleasure of agreeableness, Kant maintains, "inclination is aroused."[13] On Kant's view, inclinations are "habitual desires" that are closely connected with powerful passions which, if allowed to develop in us, constitute a significant hindrance to morality.[14] In the *Essay on the Maladies of the Head*, for example, Kant describes passions as inclinations which are of a particularly "high degree."[15] And, in the *Anthropology*, he claims that many of the passions to which we are susceptible belong to one of four categories.[16] The first is the category "mania for honour," which involves a "striving after the reputation of honour," even though the sought after reputation has nothing to do with our inner moral worth.[17] The second category is "mania for revenge," which Kant takes to involve the specific passion of hatred insofar as it arises out of an injustice we have experienced.[18] Next, there is "mania for domination," which involves placing "the advantage of force" over others.[19] Finally, there is "mania for possession," or the desire to accumulate wealth for its own sake.

A passion amounts to a hindrance to us as moral agents, on Kant's account, because, regardless of the category to which it belongs, it is at bottom an inclination that threatens to take over the mind and cloud our freedom to select among principles in acting. As he puts it in the *Metaphysics of Morals*, in passion the mind becomes fixated on a sensible desire in such a way as to form "principles upon it."[20] When a passion takes hold in the mind, it comes to ground our action in a very rigid way. The trouble with this is not that passions are connected with principles, as such – principles are essential to moral agency. Rather, the trouble with passions is that, because the relevant principles are grounded in sensible inclinations, it is possible to be rigidly drawn into acting contrary to duty. This is why Kant claims that passions may lead us to "take up what is evil (as something premeditated)" into the maxims that underlie our actions.[21] In the end, Kant claims in the *Lectures on Pedagogy*, "[i]f one wants to form a good character, one must first clear away the passions."[22]

Because the pleasure of agreeableness is a sensory pleasure that arouses inclinations, thereby paving the way for the development of passions, Kant deems this pleasure unhelpful to us insofar as we wish to develop morally. We have already begun to see that Kant finds it appropriate to differentiate between pleasures of the senses and the more refined pleasure of beauty, and it is worth noting that, in doing this, Kant is by no means alone. For example, Shaftesbury claimed in his *Characteristics*, first published in 1711, that while we are experiencing beauty, we must not be concerned with the sensory enjoyment that the object is able to offer us. He considers a case in which someone observing trees longs "for nothing so much as to taste some delicious fruit of theirs" and returns to them as a source of enjoyment whenever he is in the garden.[23] This "sordidly luxurious" delight could not, according to Shaftesbury, be the delight of beauty. Similarly, in *A Philosophical Enquiry into the Origin of Our Ideas of the Sublime and Beautiful*, published in 1757, Edmund Burke claimed that in experiencing the pleasure of beauty, we do not lust after the object that pleases us. Lust is "an energy of the mind, that hurries us on to the possession of certain objects." Whereas lower pleasures are connected with lust, beauty, the more refined pleasure, is connected with love. Beauty, Burke held, is the quality in bodies "by which they cause love, or some passion similar to it."[24] Kant was familiar with these ideas, and endorsed them in principle – even if he develops them in unique ways in his own aesthetic theory.

There is much more to Kant's defense of aesthetic pleasure against Rousseauian anti-aestheticism than is apparent so far. Merely focusing on the possibility that the arts amount to luxurious diversions offering a pleasure that is more refined than the pleasure of agreeableness would not fully capture the spirit of Kantian aesthetics. For one thing, Kant's aesthetic theory is not primarily a theory about beauty in the arts. Some of his remarks, which we will consider later, even give the impression that he is of the view that it is more difficult for us to have genuine experiences of beauty in response to artworks than in response to natural objects. Although he does in the end find a place in his theory for such experiences of artistic beauty, experiences of natural beauty fit most easily within the theory.

There are two relevant features of Kant's conception of the experience of beauty on which we will focus: its ability to cultivate in us the capacity to feel love, and its feature of being disinterested. Much of

Kant's fuller explanation as to why the pleasure of beauty can contribute to our moral development rests on the claim that it has these features.

Kant's most direct allusion to the first feature occurs in Section 29 of the third *Critique*. The pleasure of beauty, he claims, is "final in reference to the moral feeling," because it "prepares us to love something, even nature, apart from any interest."[25] Kant mentions the second feature of the pleasure of beauty in Section 59 of the third *Critique*, where he writes that "[t]aste makes, as it were, the transition from the charm of sense to habitual moral interest possible without too violent a leap," and it does this to the extent that it "teaches us to find, even in sensuous objects, a free delight apart from any charm of sense."[26] Kant's view is that the pleasure of beauty is disinterested in such a way that it can teach us to step back from inclinations relating to objects of the senses. We learn how to be pleased by things without also becoming attached to them in selfish ways. As he puts it in a reflection, the beautiful "must betray no alien interest, but please apart from any self-interest."[27]

There is, of course, a second aesthetic pleasure that Kant takes up – the pleasure of sublimity. His view is that, like the pleasure of beauty, the pleasure of sublimity is connected with a kind of emotional experience that is relevant to our moral development. Whereas the experience of beauty is connected with love, the experience of sublimity is connected with respect or esteem. The pleasure of sublimity, he claims in Section 29, is "final" for the moral feeling insofar as it prepares us "to esteem something highly even in opposition to our (sensuous) interest."[28]

Kant does not fully express the connections between aesthetic pleasure's possessing these features, and its capacity to foster our moral development. We will need to reconstruct and make explicit these connections in order properly to understand the deeper Kantian response to the anti-aesthetic thought of a philosopher such as Rousseau – and, more generally, to see how Kant's ethical priorities interact with his account of aesthetic pleasure. This is the task that we will take up in the following chapters.

It is worth highlighting that the emphasis here is on Kant's views on the moral implications of the pursuit of *aesthetic pleasure*. However, Kant also entertains various other possible connections between morality and taste which concern less directly the ethical implications of pursuing pleasure, as such. In Section 42 of the third *Critique*, for instance, he claims that if we take an interest in beautiful natural objects, this is an indication that we have an interest in morality. As he puts it, there is reason to presume the presence of "at least the germ of a good moral disposition in the case of a man to whom the beauty of nature is a matter of immediate interest."[29] Kant accepts this view partly because he maintains that there is an analogy between moral and aesthetic judgments, and he takes it to follow from this that individuals who are interested in the latter can be expected also to be interested in the former. He also has a further reason for accepting the view. When we experience a natural object as beautiful, he maintains, it feels to us as if it were designed to meet the aims of our cognitive capacities. If we have an interest in morality, moreover, we apparently seek messages of hope that the moral progress that we seek is possible given the structure of the natural world.[30] But experiencing nature as conducive to our cognitive aims in an experience of beauty can enable us to feel precisely that nature is on our side – a thought that can inspire us to continue to maintain our moral hope. That is, we may feel as if natural beauty is "the cypher in which nature speaks to us figuratively."[31]

Although these may ultimately turn out to be interesting proposals, we will leave them aside, and focus instead on the features of aesthetic pleasure, itself, that help us to develop morally by becoming better able to distance ourselves from our inclinations.[32]

The Disposition to Choose Nothing But Good Ends

The notion of "culture" plays a central role in Kant's philosophy, including his aesthetics, even if at times it plays its role unassumingly in the background. As mentioned at the beginning of the present chapter, Kant is concerned to understand how the pursuit of aesthetic pleasure might be a means by which we can pursue culture.

The process of culture, considered at the individual level, is a process of development that is divided into stages, according to Kant. In the *Lectures on Pedagogy*, he describes four main stages of culture: discipline, skill, prudence, and moralization. Discipline, he holds, is "merely the taming of savagery"; at this stage, we must be helped to reason by others, who will impose order upon our actions in order to "seek to prevent animality from doing damage to humanity."[33] Next, once our "animality" has been suitably disciplined, our skill may be developed. Skill is a capacity for procuring what we need to survive and to garner basic enjoyments in life. It is, as Kant puts it, "a faculty which is sufficient for the carrying out of whatever purpose."[34] Kant's view is that skill should be developed so that it is "thorough and not superficial," which partly means that "one must not assume the appearance of knowing things that later one cannot bring about."[35] Next, at the stage of prudence, we develop our manners and other social capacities. We become "well suited" for human society, "popular, and influential."[36] At the stage of prudence, we are becoming "civilized." However, even prudential action can be largely determined by inclinations, according to Kant, and in this sense such action is still fairly closely connected with instinct. It is not until we reach the final stage of culture, that of moralization (*Moralisirung*), that we begin to become adept at choosing "good ends" for our actions, where these amount to ends which are "necessarily approved by everyone and which can be the simultaneous ends of everyone."[37]

According to Kant, our progressing through the stages of culture occurs alongside the development of our reason. We are not, in Kant's view, born with our reason fully developed. We begin merely with a capacity to develop into rationally sophisticated beings. Reason, Kant maintains, still "needs attempts, practice and instruction in order gradually to progress from one stage of insight to another."[38] Ultimately, carrying out actions from duty – those with full moral worth – will occur near the higher end of this developmental sequence, since moral action goes hand in hand with rational sophistication. It is through the use of reason that we are able to contemplate and act on the basis of principles of duty.

Kant categorizes the stages of culture slightly differently in different works, but these characterizations have in common a tendency to frame the issue of individual development as embodying a transition away from "animality."[39] Kant understands that there is a sense in which a human being is inescapably an animal, no matter how far he or she pursues culture. But Kant believes that it is possible to distinguish between animal aspects of human beings and non-animal aspects. It is a human being's reason, specifically, that Kant takes to exemplify the part of a human being that is furthest from his or her animal nature. The contrast between humanity and animality, in fact, is implicit even in Kant's definition of "reason." In the *Idea for a Universal History*, for example, Kant claims that "reason" is "a faculty of extending the rules and aims of the use of all its powers far beyond natural instinct."[40] Whereas animals act merely on natural instinct, human beings can do more than this.

Distancing ourselves from our animality consists partly in acquiring the capacity to distance ourselves from our inclinations. This is why Kant takes moralization to be the final stage of culture, and also the stage in which the human being exemplifies most fully, and is able to live on the basis of, a split between animality and rationality. In the *Metaphysics of Morals*, Kant considers the case of a man who is initially determined to follow his inclinations, and faces a choice between satisfying his own personal needs and caring for a sick father. This man "proves his freedom in the highest degree" if he manages to put aside his inclination in order to take what he believes to be the right course of action.[41] We can say that this man is acting with a preference for his rationality.

Thus, Kant holds that we need to develop our capacity to distance ourselves from our inclinations if we wish to develop as human beings and moral agents. As Kant puts it in the Appendix to the Critique of Teleological Judgment, this distancing will amount to a kind of "negative culture." It is "negative" insofar as it functions to remove obstacles to "the *will* in its determination and choice of its ends."[42] Negative culture consists in the "liberation of the will from the despotism of desires whereby, in our attachment to certain natural things, we are rendered incapable of exercising a choice of our own."[43] Our "natural capacities," Kant writes, are "very purposively adapted to the performance of our essential functions as an animal species, but the inclinations are a great impediment to the development of our humanity." The task we face is "to prevail over the rudeness and violence of inclinations that belong more to the animal part of our nature and are most inimical to education that would fit us for our higher vocation (inclinations toward enjoyment), and to make way for the development of our humanity."[44]

It is worth noting that we need not presuppose Kant's view that it is appropriate to disparage the "animal" aspects of ourselves, as such, in the reconstruction of the account that follows. Beginning a reconstruction of Kant's aesthetics on such a controversial premise is best avoided if possible. And it is possible to do so. It is inessential to invoke the notion of "animality" in order to capture what is essential to his account of moral development by means of the pursuit of aesthetic pleasure.

That is, we can make perfectly good sense of the idea of a process of development by which we acquire the capacity to distance ourselves from inclinations without describing this process as amounting to a transition away from what is "animal" in us. While it is important to recognize that Kant is motivated to pursue connections between aesthetic pleasure and moral development partly because he holds a very specific conception of culture, only certain core elements of that account of culture are actually required to articulate the relevant connections.

Kant's account of moral development interacts with other aspects of his ethical theory in complex ways, and it will be helpful to outline, however briefly, the nature of this interaction. The concept of duty is central to Kant's ethics, and, on his view, there is certainly a sense in which we are expected to do our moral duties. But, at the same time, Kant acknowledges that we are imperfect and developing moral agents. Insofar as we are not fully developed, there is also a sense in which we cannot be expected to be capable of doing our moral duties in every particular case, especially in the face of powerful inclinations leading us away from duty.

At first glance, this picture can seem contradictory, and we need some way of making sense of it. To begin with, one difference between well developed and less developed moral agents is that the former are skilled at acting not merely *in conformity with* duty, but also *from* duty. This is a distinction between, on the one hand, merely choosing good ends, and, on the other hand, having the right motivation behind our choice of good ends. Actions done merely in conformity with duty will have the outward appearance of being dutiful, but will lack moral worth. For example, the shopkeeper whom Kant considers in the *Groundwork* may choose not to overcharge inexperienced customers, which is what duty requires. Thus, he acts in conformity with duty. However, it does not follow from the fact that his action conforms with duty that he has acted in this way "from duty and basic principles of honesty."[45] He may, for instance, merely be acting on the basis of a principle of self-love, such as one bound up with the expectation that, by maintaining a good reputation within his community, his business will do better in the long run. If he does act merely on the basis of such a principle, then his action lacks moral worth. The case in the *Groundwork* of the philanthropist further illustrates this underlying point. This philanthropist helps others merely on the basis of a feeling of sympathy and a desire to enjoy the pleasure he takes in spreading joy and satisfying others. However, he does not also understand that it is his moral duty to help others. For this reason, Kant maintains, his action lacks moral worth and is "on the same footing with other inclinations."[46]

Kant describes agents who are very highly skilled at acting from duty as possessing "virtue." Virtuous agents will be at the pinnacle of moral development. Kant holds that virtue is a kind of inner strength that manifests itself in a disposition to act from duty. Thus, in the *Metaphysics of Morals*, he describes virtue as the strength "of a human being's maxims in fulfilling his duty,"[47] and as "the moral strength of a *human being's* will in fulfilling his *duty*, a moral *constraint* through his own lawgiving reason, insofar as this constitutes itself an authority *executing* the law."[48] And in *Religion Within the Boundaries of Mere Reason*, he describes virtue as a "firmly grounded disposition to fulfill one's duty strictly."[49] Virtue is a disposition not just for choosing good ends in the face of the influence of the inclinations, but for doing so in a way that is guided by an awareness of the moral law. It is a disposition to act not just in conformity with duty, but to do so from duty.

It is important for Kantian ethics to incorporate the notion of virtue as a disposition to act from duty, since this makes possible some important distinctions. For it is possible that we should carry out our actions from duty – even all of our actions – while still lacking a morally relevant quality. As Kant points out, we may live long and guiltless lives simply as a result of having been fortunate to have escaped temptations that would have drawn us away from morally worthy action.[50] For every moral test that we have faced, we might have passed it by acting from duty. But there are many moral tests that we have not faced, perhaps because of the circumstances in which we find ourselves. If we were born into a privileged social position, for example, we might not be tempted to steal; or, if we have become entrenched in certain habits of action that have come to seem necessary, we may never fully realize that we *could* act contrary to duty and on the basis of principles of self-love if we so chose.[51] To the extent that we have been able to act from duty primarily because of our good fortune rather than out of a stable disposition to do so in a variety of counterfactual scenarios, we may be said to lack virtue.[52]

Thus, consider three cases involving philanthropists. The first is that of the philanthropist considered earlier. Although he succeeds in acting in conformity with duty – which is in itself an achievement – his actions still lack moral worth, since they do not emanate from a recognition of his duty. A second philanthropist chooses to help others out of a sense of duty in all the scenarios he actually faces. But were he faced with more difficult moral tests, he would choose to disregard the duty to help others and choose instead to act on principles of self-love. This second philanthropist succeeds in acting in conformity with duty as well as from duty, but ultimately lacks virtue. By contrast, a third philanthropist acts both in conformity with duty and from duty in the cases he actually faces, and also would carry out philanthropic acts from duty in a wide range of non-actual cases which would challenge his moral resolve. Only this third philanthropist deserves to be called virtuous.

Even though the gold standard for moral action is to be virtuous, and thus to be capable of acting from duty on a consistent basis, Kant's view admits of degrees of moral development. His view even allows us to say that individuals who manage to act in conformity with duty without also acting from duty are doing better than individuals who do not even manage to act in conformity with duty. In fact, this is exactly what Kant believes. He views it as an achievement when we develop to the point of being able to act in conformity with duty, given that we all face inclinations that tempt us away from doing even this much. In the *Metaphysics of Morals*, for instance, Kant describes sympathetic joy and sadness as "sensible feelings of pleasure or pain ... at another's state of joy or sorrow," and claims that the capacity to feel sympathy is "one of the impulses that nature has implanted in us to do what representations of duty alone might not accomplish."[53] Even though, as his treatment of the original philanthropist case makes clear, Kant holds that, in acting in conformity with duty by drawing on a feeling of sympathy but not on a principle of duty, our action does not have full moral worth, it is still true that we have accomplished something worthwhile. We have at least acted in conformity with duty, when we might have failed to do so.

Similarly, in the *Anthropology*, Kant describes the role of the feeling of compassion in moral agency. He contrasts compassion, which he describes as an inclination "of pathological (sensible) impulse," with the state of moral apathy which he takes to characterize wise individuals, and to be an "entirely correct and sublime moral principle of the Stoic school." On the one hand, Kant claims, the virtuous or wise individual "must never be in a state of affect, not even in that of compassion with the misfortune of his best friend," and this is because affect "makes us (more or less) blind."[54] Yet, on the other hand, the reality is that we do have a tendency to feel compassion, and there is no reason for us to avoid making use of this tendency in order to bring ourselves to act in conformity with duty. As Kant puts it, "[t]he wisdom of nature has planted in us the predisposition to compassion in order to handle the reins *provisionally*, until reason has achieved the necessary strength; that is to say, for the purpose of enlivening us, nature has added the incentive of pathological (sensible) impulse to the moral incentives for the good, as a temporary surrogate of reason."[55]

We can now make better sense of what seemed to be a tension in Kant's ethical thought. It is true that there is a sense in which we cannot be expected to be capable of doing our moral duties in every particular case. We are not born embodying the wisdom that Kant attributes to the Stoic; we are not born with the developed capacity consistently to act from duty. As such, there are bound to be cases in which we will falter, morally. On the other hand, there remains a sense in which we ought to do our moral duties. To say this is to say that we ought to do what it takes to make ourselves into the kinds of people who can consistently act from duty. Given that learning to act in conformity with duty on a consistent basis is a first step in learning to act from duty, we may pursue our task partly by learning how better to act in conformity with duty. This is why Kant claims that we have, for instance, an "indirect duty" to cultivate "the compassionate natural (aesthetic) feelings in us, and to make use of them as so many means to sympathy based on moral principles and the feeling appropriate to them." Cultivating our capacity for sympathy is one way for us to develop morally by learning to act in conformity with duty. We may cultivate the relevant compassionate feelings in us, Kant suggests, by placing ourselves in circumstances in which we will be able to share in painful feelings that we find difficult to resist, including circumstances in which we interact with those living in poverty or with illnesses.[56]

Most relevant in the present context is a second way of pursuing moral development. This, of course, is the pursuit of aesthetic pleasure. It is clear that Kant takes this pursuit to be one way of pursuing a process of culture that will help us to learn to distance ourselves from our inclinations, and in so doing to help us to become more sophisticated moral agents.[57] As he puts in the Critique of Teleological Judgment, the arts "do much to overcome the tyrannical propensities of the senses, and so prepare man for a sovereignty in which reason alone shall have sway."[58] Pursuing aesthetic pleasure will help us to acquire skill in putting aside our inclinations in order to act in conformity with duty, but will not directly teach us to act from duty. From a Kantian point of view, though, even this is an achievement.[59]

Although we are focusing on Kantian moral theory, one does not need to accept such a moral theory in order to endorse Kant's account of the connection between aesthetic pleasure and the loosening of inclinations. And it goes without saying that achieving such a loosening will constitute a moral achievement from the point of view of various non-Kantian moral theories – including those which do not even consider whether a given action was done from duty in determining its moral worth.

Notes

1 Jean-Jacques Rousseau, *"The Discourses" and Other Early Political Writings*, ed. Victor Gourevitch (Cambridge: Cambridge University Press, 1997), 11n.
2 Ethics 27:396.
3 Ethics 27:248.
4 Ethics 27:248.
5 Ethics 27:394.
6 Ethics 27:396–397. See also the Appendix to the "Critique of Teleological Judgment," where Kant seems directly to reference Rousseau's views on the arts and sciences, claiming that "[t]he preponderance of evil which a taste refined to the extreme of idealization, and which even luxury in the sciences, considered as food for vanity, diffuses among us as the result of the crowd of insatiable inclinations which they beget, is indisputable" (CJ 5:433–434).
7 Ethics 27:396–397.
8 Ethics 27:394–395.
9 Anthropology 7:237.
10 CJ 5:209.
11 CJ 5:207.
12 CJ 5:209.
13 CJ 5:207.
14 Morals 6:212.
15 Maladies 2:261.

16 In the *Anthropology*, Kant distinguishes between passions resulting from human culture (those involving honor, revenge, domination, and possession), and "natural" or "innate" passions – which include the inclinations for freedom and sex (Anthropology 7:267–268).

17 Anthropology 7:272.

18 Anthropology 7:270.

19 Anthropology 7:273.

20 Morals 6:408.

21 Morals 6:408. Similarly, Kant claims in the *Anthropology* that passions are not merely "unfortunate states of mind full of many ills," but are "without exception evil as well" (Anthropology 7:267).

22 Pedagogy 9:486-487. Along these lines, Kant claims in the unpublished "first introduction" to the third *Critique* that inclinations come in degrees, and that what is needed is "moderation of the inclinations in order not to yield to passion" (FI 196).

23 Anthony Ashley Cooper, Third Earl of Shaftesbury, *Characteristics of Men, Manners, Opinions, Times* (Cambridge: Cambridge University Press, 1999), 319.

24 Edmund Burke, *A Philosophical Enquiry into the Origin of Our Ideas of the Sublime and Beautiful* (Oxford: Oxford University Press, 2008), 83.

25 CJ 5:267.

26 CJ 5:354.

27 Reflections 827, 15:310.

28 CJ 5:267.

29 CJ 5:301.

30 For more on this aspect of Kant's view, see Heiner Bielefeldt, *Symbolic Representation in Kant's Practical Philosophy* (Cambridge: Cambridge University Press, 2003), 124.

31 CJ 5:301.

32 When it comes to connections between Kant's aesthetics and ethics, generally speaking, Paul Guyer distinguishes between aesthetic phenomena that play a role in "moral epistemology," and those that play a role in "moral psychology." In the case of moral epistemology, Guyer claims, Kant's view is that the "aesthetic experience of the freedom of the imagination in the response to beauty and of the power of reason in the feeling of the sublime can make our practical freedom palpable to us, thus supplementing the entirely nonexperiential inference of our freedom from our obligation under the moral law" (*Kant and the Experience of Freedom* [Cambridge: Cambridge University Press, 1996], 335; see also *Values of Beauty* [Cambridge: Cambridge University Press, 2005], ch. 8). For instance, Kant claims in Section 59 of the third *Critique* that beauty is a symbol of the morally

good, for the reason that there are allegedly structural similarities between aesthetic and moral judgment. Thus, judging aesthetically might reveal to us the freedom we have as moral agents. Much of the secondary literature on connections between Kant's aesthetics and ethics focuses on moral epistemology. See, for example, Henry Allison, *Kant's Theory of Taste: A Reading of the Critique of Aesthetic Judgment* (Cambridge: Cambridge University Press, 2001), part III; Kenneth Rogerson, *The Problem of Free Harmony in Kant's Aesthetics* (Albany: SUNY Press, 2008), ch. 6; Rachel Zuckert, *Kant on Beauty and Biology* (Cambridge: Cambridge University Press, 2007), 370–383; Rodolphe Gasché, *The Idea of Form: Rethinking Kant's Aesthetics* (Stanford: Stanford University Press, 2003), 158–165; and Donald Crawford, *Kant's Aesthetic Theory* (Madison: University of Wisconsin Press), ch. 7. By contrast, the focus in what follows is instead on moral psychology, and specifically on the moral psychological implications of the experience of aesthetic pleasure. Guyer is one commentator who does find it worthwhile to address these issues, as he does, for instance, in *Kant and the Experience of Freedom*. We also find brief references to them in G. Felicitas Munzel, *Kant's Conception of Moral Character: the "Critical" Link of Morality, Anthropology, and Reflective Judgment* (Chicago: University of Chicago Press, 1999), 297–300; and Allen Wood, *Kant's Ethical Thought* (Cambridge: Cambridge University Press, 1999), 393.

33 Pedagogy 9:449.

34 Anthropology 7:201. Cf. Pedagogy 9:449.

35 Pedagogy 9:486.

36 Pedagogy 9:450. In the *Anthropology*, Kant adds that acquiring these social skills partly involves becoming adept at "using other human beings for one's purposes" (Anthropology 7:201).

37 Pedagogy 9:450. When our capacities are developed to the point of prudence, we can be said to be civilized. But, according to Kant, no matter how civilized we have become, "very much is still lacking before we can be held to be already moralized" (Idea 8:26).

38 Idea 8:19. See Thomas Pogge, "Kant on Ends and the Meaning of Life," in *Reclaiming the History of Ethics: Essays for John Rawls*, ed. Andrews Reath, Barbara Herman, and Christine M. Korsgaard (Cambridge: Cambridge University Press, 1997), 381.

39 In the *Anthropology*, Kant describes the stages in the development of reason as consisting in "skill," "prudence," and "wisdom." There, he suggests that this development can be tied to chronological age: "The age at which the human being reaches the full use of his reason can be fixed, in respect to his skill (the capacity to achieve any purpose one chooses), around the twentieth year; in respect to prudence (using other human beings for one's

purposes), around the fortieth year; and finally, in respect to wisdom, around the sixtieth year. However, in this last period wisdom is more negative; it sees the follies of the first two periods. At this point we can say: 'It is too bad that we have to die now, just when we have learned for the very first time how we should have lived quite well'" (Anthropology 7:201).

In the *Religion* Kant distinguishes among three ways in which the "predisposition to good in human nature" may be determined: "[t] he predisposition to the animality of the human being, as a living being ... [t]o the humanity in him, as a living and at the same time rational being ... [and] [t]o his personality, as a rational and at the same time responsible being" (Religion 6:26). In the *Lectures on Pedagogy*, it should be noted, Kant also finds it helpful to employ an additional distinction, between "physical" and "practical" culture. He takes the latter to divide into "pragmatic" and "moral" culture (Pedagogy 9:470).

40 Idea 8:18.

41 Morals 6:382n.

42 CJ 5:431.

43 CJ 5:432.

44 CJ 5:433. Kant makes a similar point in the *Groundwork*, writing that "[t]he human being feels within himself a powerful counterweight to all the commands of duty, which reason represents to him as so deserving of the highest respect – the counterweight of his needs and inclinations" (Groundwork 4:405). And in the *Metaphysics of Morals*, he writes that human beings are "rational *natural* beings, who are unholy enough that pleasure can induce them to break the moral law, even though they recognize its authority" (Morals 6:379). Because we are tempted away from morality by our inclinations, we are unlike hypothetical "holy" beings, who, lacking a sensible nature, would not face the prospect of being drawn away from the moral law by inclinations. Such holy beings would not face the need to master inclinations that "rebel against the law," in the first place (Morals 6:383).

45 Groundwork 4:397.

46 Groundwork 4:398.

47 Morals 6:394.

48 Morals 6:405.

49 Religion 6:23–24n.

50 Morals 6:392–393.

51 Morals 6:407.

52 For a similar interpretation, see Philip Stratton-Lake, "Being Virtuous and the Virtues: Two Aspects of Kant's Doctrine of Virtue," in *Kant's Ethics of Virtue*, ed. Monika Betzler (Berlin: Walter de Gruyter, 2008), 104.

53 Morals 6:456–457.

54   Anthropology 7:253.
55   Anthropology 7:253.
56   Morals 6:457. More generally, Kant holds that the *"cultivation* of any *capacities* whatever for furthering ends set forth by reason" is a duty of wide obligation (Morals 6:391). This is a "wide" duty in the sense that it is bound up with "playroom (*latitudo*) for free choice in following (complying with) the law" (Morals 6:390), and "[n]o rational principle prescribes specifically *how* far one should go in cultivating one's capacities (in enlarging or correcting one's capacity for understanding, i.e., in acquiring knowledge or skill)." Instead, "different situations in which human beings may find themselves make a human being's choice of the occupation for which he should cultivate his talents very much a matter for him to decide as he chooses" (Morals 6:392). Cf. Groundwork 4:424.
57   Guyer takes up this issue in *Kant and the Experience of Freedom*, where he recognizes that in Kant's ethics, principles interact with feelings, which are susceptible to cultivation by various means – including by means of aesthetic pursuits (ch. 10).
58   CJ 5:433–434.
59   In what follows, we will be concerned with Kant's conception of culture in the very specific sense that has just been outlined. At times, Kant uses terms whose English translation is "culture" (including *Kultur* and *Bildung*) in ways that diverge from the specific sense that is primarily of interest here. It is beyond the scope of the present study to trace the subtle nuances of his usage of these terms, or to examine how Kant's views on culture fit into the tradition of theorizing culture that was emerging in Germany around the time that Kant lived – and which involved writers such as Mendelssohn, Schiller, and Goethe. For more on this topic, see Nathan Rotenstreich, "Morality and Culture: A Note on Kant," *History of Philosophy Quarterly* 6, no. 3 (1989): 303–316; Susan Cocalis, "The Transformation of 'Bildung' From an Image to an Ideal," *Monatshefte* 70, no. 4 (1978): 399–414; Hans-Georg Gadamer, *Truth and Method* (London: Continuum, 2004), 8–17; and W. H. Bruford, *The German Tradition of Self-Cultivation: "Bildung" from Humboldt to Thomas Mann* (Cambridge: Cambridge University Press, 2010).

2

Beauty and Love

A Need of Being Grateful

Beauty, Kant claims in Section 29 of the third *Critique*, is "final" in reference to moral feeling, because it "prepares us to love something, even nature, apart from any interest."[1] Other than this remark, Kant says very little about the connection between beauty, love, and moral development.

To make a start at understanding what sort of connection he has in mind, we can note that he is not unique in thinking that beauty and love are somehow connected. As previously mentioned, Burke's view is that beauty is the quality in bodies which causes us to feel love toward them; love, unlike lust, involves no desire to possess the object. A key feature of such an account is that the feeling of love is directed toward the object that we find beautiful. It is possible, then, that Kant is claiming here that the experience of beauty prepares us to love the object apart from interest.

Kant does indicate that he believes it to be possible for us to feel love toward the objects we find beautiful, even those which are inanimate. He indicates this, for instance, in the remark just mentioned: the experience of beauty prepares us to love "even nature" apart from interest. Similarly, in the *Metaphysics of Morals*, he describes the possibility of

The Possibility of Culture: Pleasure and Moral Development in Kant's Aesthetics,
First Edition. Bradley Murray.
© 2015 John Wiley & Sons, Inc. Published 2015 by John Wiley & Sons, Inc.

loving "beautiful crystal formations" and "the indescribable beauty of plants" apart from an intention to use these.[2] Thus, perhaps Kant's view is that feeling love toward the natural and artistic objects we find beautiful provides us with an opportunity to cultivate our capacity to love, more generally. Given, moreover, that having the capacity to love can help us to develop the morally relevant capacity to distance ourselves from our inclinations, it is open to us to pursue experiences of beauty as a means of developing morally.

Even if this is part of the story, however, it is not the whole story – and it is likely not the most important part of the story. For Kant is hesitant in accepting Burke's strategy of assigning a prominent role to the feeling of love toward the object in an explanation of the pleasure of beauty. Kant holds, instead, that the feeling of love can at most be incidental. Speaking of Burke's explanation, Kant writes: "[t]he beautiful, which he grounds on love (from which, still, he would have desire kept separate), he reduces to 'the relaxing, slackening, and enervating of the fibres of the body, and consequently a softening, a dissolving, a languor, and a fainting, dying, and melting away for pleasure.'"[3] The trouble with Burke's view, according to Kant, is that, if we attribute the delight in the object "wholly and entirely to the gratification which it affords through charm or emotion," then it follows that "we must not expect from *anyone else* agreement with the aesthetic judgement passed by *us*."[4] If the pleasure of beauty were grounded merely in an emotion of love that we feel toward the object, we would have no basis for engaging in disputes over taste. Yet, Kant thinks, it is obvious that we do have such a basis. This is why, rather than taking the feeling of love toward the object to be primary in an explanation of the pleasure of beauty, Kant takes the experience of "subjective finality" to be primary. More will be said about this in a moment. But roughly speaking, for now, the experience of subjective finality is the experience of the object's being pre-adapted to our cognitive capacities.

Ideally, a reconstruction of the connection between beauty, love, and moral development will conform to, and draw on the deeper elements of the Kantian explanation of the pleasure of beauty. And it is just such an account that we will now articulate. The account will invoke the notion of subjective finality, as well as elements of Kant's moral psychology, in order to describe a connection between beauty and love that goes by way of the emotion of *gratitude*.[5]

There is a subtle feature of the phenomenology of experiences of beauty to which Kant draws our attention, but which we might miss if we are not looking carefully. This is its close connection with the emotion of gratitude. Finding a song to be beautiful as we listen to it, finding a meadow to be beautiful as we peer upon it while walking through nature, finding a poem to be beautiful as we hear it being recited, or finding a painting or sculpture to be beautiful as we engage with it in a museum are all experiences that tend to mobilize feelings of gratitude. Kant takes up the connection between gratitude and natural beauty in a passage in the Appendix to the Critique of Teleological Judgment. When someone is "amid beautiful surroundings" and is "in calm and serene enjoyment of his existence," he "feels within him a need – a need of being grateful for it to someone."[6] The same can be said of artistic beauty: experiencing the song, poem, painting, or sculpture as beautiful gives rise to a need, however subtle, of being grateful to someone for the experience.

What is it that makes the experience of the pleasure of beauty particularly closely connected with gratitude – more so, say, than the experience of the pleasure of agreeableness? A full explanation will invoke the deeper feature of the phenomenology of the experience of beauty just mentioned – its subjective finality. We experience objects in which we take the pleasure of beauty as if they were "pre-adapted" to, or designed to fit with, our cognitive capacities.[7] Kant elucidates this notion in the Introduction to the third *Critique*, where he explores what he takes to be the analogy between the pleasure of beauty, and the pleasure that we can feel in the course of scientific investigation. While investigating the world scientifically, he claims, we come to experience nature as if it were designed for the benefit of our cognitive capacities or understanding. He describes this as an experience of nature as being "final" for our understanding, and points out that the experience can be connected with pleasure. If we discover, for example, that "two or more empirical heterogeneous laws of nature are allied under one principle that embraces them both," such a discovery can be "the ground of a very appreciable pleasure, often even of admiration, and such, too, as does not wear off even though we are already familiar enough with its object."[8] Kant's explanation of the pleasure we feel in the case of beauty mirrors his explanation of the pleasure we feel in the case of scientific discovery. That is, we feel that the object we find beautiful fits well with our cognitive capacities, and this is a pleasing feeling.[9]

It is because experiences of beauty are characterized by the feeling of subjective finality that they are closely connected with feelings of gratitude. Generally speaking, gratitude is an appropriate response when we feel that we have been given a gift by another. We feel the utmost gratitude when we are given a gift that we feel has been selected or designed just for us, a gift that suits our personality and nature nearly perfectly. Because the experience of the pleasure of beauty is characterized by subjective finality, it is as if we have been given just such a gift.

Artists skilled at creating beautiful works, it can be said, benefit us by making objects that we feel fit exquisitely with our natures. As mentioned at the outset, Kantian aesthetics is premised on the subjectivity of taste, and hence on an appreciation of the fact that it can be notoriously difficult to find universal agreement on cases of beauty in practice. But a painting such as Raphael's *Sistine Madonna*, or musical works such as Beethoven's String Quartet No. 14 in C# minor, Op. 131 and John Coltrane's *Stellar Regions*, certainly seem to evoke in many of us experiences of beauty. Similarly, a literary work such as Eliot's *Burnt Norton* seems to manifest a striking lyrical beauty. It is natural for us to feel gratitude toward these artists as we experience the beauty of their artworks. This may partly explain why we tend to elevate and revere artists who we feel to be uniquely talented in producing works of beauty, even describing them as "geniuses." As Kant puts it in the third *Critique*, we tend to think of such artists as "nature's elect – a type that must be regarded as but a rare phenomenon."[10]

Although it seems quite appropriate to speak of gratitude in connection with experiences of artistic beauty, it might seem less appropriate to speak this way in connection with experiences of natural beauty. Who, if anyone, has "made" the natural object that we experience as beautiful? Gratitude for a beautiful natural object such as a meadow would, if taken literally, seemingly need to be directed toward a representation of a divine creator – or, as Kant puts it, toward "an object that is not in the world."[11] Does this mean that finding nature to be beautiful, having the corresponding feeling of its being designed to fit our cognitive capacities, and consequently feeling a sense of gratitude is sufficient to prove that we believe in a creator, however vigorously we might otherwise deny maintaining such a belief?

Kant does not hold that experiencing natural beauty commits us to a belief in a creator. He does hold, however, that it is possible, if not common, for us all to behave at times *as if* there were a divine creator of the world. This type of thinking is an instance of what Kant calls the "regulative" employment of reason, and more will be said about it in Chapter 6. But it is clear that Kant takes this type of thinking to be both necessary and justified. Given the place of regulative uses of reason in our lives, we can expect that even those who do not believe that there is anyone who literally created the natural world to whom they can actually be grateful might, consistently with this belief, still sometimes experience spontaneous feelings of gratitude while experiencing natural beauty. We can imagine an atheist saying: "I know there is no creator of this scene of natural beauty, but right now I am very taken by it, and am feeling strong emotions – including a strange feeling of gratitude."

Compared to the experience of agreeableness, the experience of beauty will be particularly closely connected with gratitude. It is not that it is impossible that we should feel as though something in which we take sensory pleasure has been made specifically for us. If a baker makes me a cake and I am fond of it, I may experience the baker as having designed the dish to fit with my preferences, and may feel a corresponding feeling of gratitude in response. However, in experiencing an object as manifesting subjective finality, as we do in the case of beauty, the feeling is of being much more deeply understood. It is one thing to feel that someone understands our sensory preferences, and another thing altogether to feel that someone understands what will please us in a more profound way that is bound up with the very nature of our mode of cognition. This feeling that the object's actual or hypothetical maker deeply understands us characterizes the experience of beauty, but does not characterize the experience of agreeableness, on a Kantian account.

Beyond this, there is a second relevant difference between the experiences of beauty and agreeableness. In the case of beauty, the gratitude we feel can be unwavering. The feeling of subjective finality that characterizes an experience of beauty is such that it seems practically inconceivable to us that the object's actual or hypothetical maker should have designed it while also being indifferent to us, much less while being out to harm us. By contrast, the pleasure of agreeableness is, in fact, potentially harmful, and it seems entirely conceivable to us that the maker should have been indifferent toward us, or even that he or she wished to do us harm. While I may be pleased by the baker's cake, my experience of pleasure is compatible with the possibility that the baker is an enemy out to nourish a sugar addiction. Generally speaking, the feeling we have toward the maker of that which we find agreeable can easily be ambivalent or negative, and it is not a given that gratitude is warranted.

There are, Kant points out, "*three specifically different kinds of delight*," which correspond to "three different relations of representations to the feeling of pleasure and displeasure."[12] Aside from the contemplative pleasures of beauty and sublimity, and the pleasure of agreeableness, there is also the pleasure of goodness. It is worth considering how this third pleasure stands in relation to gratitude. In order to do this, we must first take a moment to consider Kant's account of goodness. He describes this pleasure in Section 5 of the third *Critique*:

> That is *good* which by means of reason commends itself by its mere concept. We call that *good for something* (useful) which only pleases as a means; but that which pleases on its own account we call *good in itself*. In both cases the concept of an end is implied, and consequently the relation of reason to (at least possible) willing, and thus a delight in the *existence* of an Object or action, i.e. some interest or other. To deem something good, I must always know what sort of a thing the object is intended to be, i.e. I must have a concept of it.[13]

The pleasure of goodness is an experience with which most of us are familiar – it is the experience of being pleased in recognizing excellent design and craftsmanship.

Kant distinguishes in this passage between two ways in which we might experience an object as manifesting goodness. In the first place, we may find it to be good in itself. In this case, we take pleasure in the design and its execution, as such, without taking pleasure in the object's serving a useful function. This is a kind of pleasure in the object's overall level of perfection. On Kant's view, an object's perfection has to do with the degree to which it lives up to the maker's original intentions for it. There are, Kant suggests, two ways in which an object can manifest perfection: qualitatively and quantitatively. Qualitative perfection amounts to "the agreement of the manifold in a thing with this concept," whereas quantitative perfection "consists in the completeness of anything after its kind, and is a mere concept of quantity (of totality)."

In the latter case, Kant claims, "the question of *what the thing is to be* is regarded as definitely disposed of, and we only ask whether it is possessed of *all* the requisites that go to make it such."[14] This invites an interpretation according to which an object's possessing qualitative perfection is simply a matter of its successfully instantiating the general sort that its maker intended it to instantiate, and that its possessing quantitative perfection is a matter of its being an exemplary instance of that sort. For example, if someone sets out to make a cabin, but ends up failing, so that there is only a pile of wood whose pieces have been fastened together using nails, then there is no sense in which the object "agrees" with the sortal concept "cabin." Such an object will lack qualitative perfection – as well, of course, as lacking quantitative perfection. On the other hand, if the maker does succeed not only in making something that instantiates the general sortal concept "cabin," but also in making an exemplary cabin, then the object will possess both qualitative and quantitative perfection.

In addition to the possibility of being pleased because we find the object to be good in itself, or to manifest perfection, we may also be pleased because we find it to be good for something, or, in other words, to be useful. For instance, I may take pleasure in the cabin because it is good at protecting me from harsh weather and wild animals. Of course, the pleasures of utility and perfection will not always be clearly separable. In cases in which the sortal concept that the object instantiates is also a functional concept, as seems to be true of the concept of a cabin, the assessment of the object's level of quantitative perfection will invoke this function. Supposing, for example, that things of the sort "cabin" are to perform the function of keeping occupants protected from weather and wild animals, then it will follow that a cabin will manifest perfection to the extent that it is capable of performing these functions.

Like the pleasure of agreeableness, the pleasure of goodness will be less closely bound up with gratitude than is the pleasure of beauty. In the case of the pleasure of perfection, the spectator is pleased upon making an intellectual judgment that the object has lived up to what it is supposed to be. However, the maker can easily be experienced as being indifferent to the object's spectators. I need not experience the maker of a well-crafted piece of furniture, say, as having acted to enable people like me to enjoy the object's perfection, since he or she might have been indifferent to our pleasure. The pleasure of utility, like the pleasure of perfection, will lack a close connection with gratitude. I may find the object to be useful, and feel pleasure as a consequence, even if I do not find the object to be useful to me. For instance, I may take pleasure in an elegantly designed and built piece of construction equipment for use in building large dams even though I may never build such a dam, or even live anywhere near one. This is not to say that I will never feel grateful to the maker of an object that I do find personally useful. It is just to say that gratitude is not closely connected with the pleasure of utility in the way that it is with the pleasure of beauty.

Uniting Gratitude with Love of Man

Once we have come to recognize how closely connected the pleasure of beauty is with the feeling of gratitude, it becomes possible to make sense of the idea that the pleasure of beauty contributes to our capacity to love.

The observation that we can cultivate love through gratitude is an aspect of an easily overlooked side of Kant's thought – namely, his artic-ulation of a moral psychology which is developmental in nature. Kant suggests, in fact, that there are two ways in which to cultivate love: by practicing either gratitude or beneficence. Let us first consider the case of beneficence. According to Kant, beneficence is a state that is connected with "the maxim of making others' happiness one's end."[15] Insofar as we act beneficently, we give to another without expecting anything in return. Kant considers the case of a wealthy individual who gives to those who are financially worse off. If this individual is truly to act beneficently, he will be careful to "avoid any appearance of intending to bind the other" by his act of giving; and, in fact, it is best if he either demonstrates that "he is himself put under obligation by the other's acceptance or hon-oured by it," or else practices his beneficence "in complete secrecy."[16] But, Kant adds, the true spirit of beneficence emerges in cases in which the benefactor is not wealthy, but rather has only limited means and is willing to endure the hardship that he or she will face as a consequence of giving to another. If someone practices beneficence often and success-fully, "he eventually comes actually to love the person he has helped." This suggests an interpretation of the saying "you ought to *love* your neighbour as yourself": it does not mean, Kant observes, "that you ought immediately (first) to love him and (afterwards) by means of this love do good to him," but rather "*do good* to your fellow human beings, and your beneficence will produce love of them in you (as an aptitude of the inclination to beneficence in general)."[17] Thus, we may cultivate feelings of love toward others by making it our practice to do good to them.[18]

It is primarily in the *Metaphysics of Morals* that Kant explores the relevant connections between gratitude and love. First, he suggests, when we feel grateful, our experience is of someone else as having favored us out of love.[19] Second, genuine gratitude also inspires in us a desire to give to others out of love. Rather than "regarding a kindness received as a burden one would gladly be rid of," one feels that there is an opportunity "to unite the virtue of gratitude with love of man, to combine the *cordiality* of a benevolent disposition with *sensitivity to benevolence* ... and so to cultivate one's love of human beings.[20] In feeling grateful, we may desire, in the first place, to give back to the benefactor. But if this individual is absent and cannot receive our services in return – perhaps because he or she is no longer living – we may instead wish to direct our feelings toward others.[21]

The picture that is emerging is one according to which the pleasure of beauty, by virtue of its close connection with gratitude, can enable us to develop the capacity to love. When we experience beauty, we feel gratitude toward an actual or hypothetical maker of the object, and this, in turn, tends to mobilize in us a desire to give to others out of love.

Subordinating One's Own Particular Inclination

That experiences of beauty contribute to our capacity to love because they afford us opportunities to feel gratitude is a compelling psychological claim. But even if it is true, we have yet to see why having the capacity to love is relevant to our moral development as individuals. We need to see, specifically, why the cultivation of this capacity can help us to distance ourselves from our inclinations.

It is clear that one conception of love – which Kant refers to as "practical" love – is not the conception that is primarily at issue in the present context. Practical love, and the related feeling of practical respect, are "feelings," in a very specific sense. A practical moral feeling, Kant claims, is "produced solely by reason."[22] By contrast, a "pathological" feeling is one that is produced by the sensible, as opposed to rational, side of our nature. Practical love, Kant claims, amounts to a feeling of "gladness" in fulfilling our moral duties. As he puts it in the *Critique of Practical Reason*, to love one's neighbor practically "means to practice all duties toward him *gladly*."[23] Practical love is not relevant here because Kant takes it to be impossible for human beings actually to feel such love. To be capable of feeling practical love, according to Kant, we must have reached the stage of actually liking to practice our moral duties. Those who had reached such a stage would no longer face inclinations tempting them to deviate from their duties. But, on Kant's view, it is impossible for any of us actually to reach such a stage. We will inevitably be faced with desires that require us to exercise self-constraint, and overcoming these desires inevitably involves "inner necessitation to what one does not altogether like to do."[24] While it is necessary for us to make "mere love for the law" the "constant though unattainable goal" of our striving, our motivation to act from duty can only derive from a sterner feeling of respect.

A second conception of love, namely, that of pathological love, is more relevant to the present discussion. We can better understand Kant's conception of this kind of love if we look to the *Observations*. As he describes it there, pathological love is a kind of "universal affection," a feeling that "spreads further" than other affectionate feelings. It involves subordinating one's own particular inclination to an enlarged one.[25] Such love is the least self-interested of affectionate feelings, and, on the moral theory of the *Observations*, leads to virtuous actions.[26] Only when one "subordinates one's own particular inclination to such an enlarged one," Kant writes, "can our kindly drives be proportionately applied and bring about the noble attitude that is the beauty of virtue."[27] Given Kant's later distinction between actions done in conformity with duty, and actions also done from duty, we can say that actions proceeding from pathological love will tend to conform with duty, even if they are not done from duty. As already emphasized, however, it is a moral achievement even to be capable of putting aside inclinations in order to act in conformity with duty. Thus, cultivating the capacity for pathological love goes hand in hand with moral development.

Kant suggests in the *Observations* that sympathy, which he there describes as a feeling of "kindly participation in the fate of other people," is usefully considered alongside the feeling of pathological love.[28] Love, Kant claims, is like sympathy that has been made slightly "colder" and that has been "raised to its proper universality."[29] Sympathy remains "weak" and "blind," causing our hearts to "swell with tenderness on behalf of every human being and swim in melancholy for everyone else's need."[30] As such, it can lead us away from taking up the more impartial stance that typically grounds our capacity to act in morally right ways. Kant considers an example in which a person who owes money to someone else is moved by a feeling of sympathy toward a third person in need, and decides to give money to this needy person instead of paying his own debt. The trouble, according to Kant, is that, in giving to the needy person, the first person is overcome by the "blind enchantment" of his or her feeling of sympathy, and consequently fails to "fulfill the strict duty of justice." The key difference between being motivated by a feeling of sympathy, on the one hand, and by the more sophisticated feeling of love, on the other hand, is precisely that the latter is less bound up with inclinations that restrict its universality. Only pathological love is bound up with "general affection towards humankind."[31] Still, in making it possible for us to carry out "beautiful actions that would perhaps all be suffocated by the preponderance of a cruder self-interest," sympathy can be helpful to us as we develop our capacities to feel love.[32]

We can illustrate the moral difference that the capacity to feel pathological love makes by returning to the case that Kant considers in the *Metaphysics of Morals* in which a man faces a choice between satisfying his own personal inclination and caring for a sick father. This man "proves his freedom in the highest degree" insofar as he manages to put aside his inclination in order to do what he believes to be the right course of action.[33] However, given this person's current level of moral development, he may not be in a position so easily to put aside his inclination. How might he develop to be able to do this? One way will be to cultivate his capacity to feel pathological love. Once he is capable of loving, he will be capable of being moved by his feeling of universal affection to consider others' needs – including his father's – alongside his own. And one way to bring himself to this level of moral development will be to pursue experiences of beauty. Pursuing beauty will be helpful to him because it will provide him with the opportunity to feel a deep, transformative, feeling of gratitude. Speaking more generally, we can say, as Kant does, that beauty "prepares us to love" apart from any interest.[34]

Notes

1   CJ 5:267.
2   Morals 6:443.
3   CJ 5:277.
4   CJ 5:278.
5   In drawing extensively on the details of Kant's moral psychology, the present interpretation of the passage under consideration differs from other interpretations. For instance, Rudolph Gasché's interpretation is based primarily on the premise that the experience of beauty is characterized by disinterestedness, as is the feeling of love, and that it is because these share disinterestedness in common that judgments of beauty amount to "intimations of moral feeling" (*The Idea of Form: Rethinking Kant's Aesthetics* (Stanford: Stanford University Press, 2003), 161–162).
6   CJ 5:445.
7   Many commentators interpret the notion of subjective finality in a similar way. Paul Guyer suggests that Kant holds that an object we find beautiful pleases "in reference to a more general aim on the part of subjects – the aim of cognition itself, on which Kant's entire theory of aesthetic response depends" (*Kant and the Claims of Taste* [Cambridge: Cambridge University Press, 1997], 192). Kenneth Rogerson claims that Kant's view is that the appreciation of natural beauty involves "noticing that objects are organized in such a way as to satisfy the purpose of reflective judgment" (*The Problem of Free Harmony in Kant's Aesthetics* [Albany: SUNY Press, 2008], 51). Rachel Zuckert takes Kant to claim that we appreciate a beautiful object in virtue of its form, and that we "take pleasure in such form because it is purposive, as if designed for our representation of it" (*Kant on Beauty and Biology* [Cambridge: Cambridge University Press, 2007], 186). See also Thomas Pogge, "Kant on Ends and the Meaning of Life," in *Reclaiming the History of Ethics: Essays for John Rawls*, ed. Andrews Reath, Barbara Herman, and Christine M. Korsgaard (Cambridge: Cambridge University Press, 1997), 367–368.

It is worth noting that, contrasting with these interpretations as well as the present one, Henry Allison's interpretation emphasizes a different dimension of subjective finality. Rather than emphasizing the sense in which the *object* is subjectively final insofar as it is experienced as fitting with our cognitive capacities, Allison seeks to establish that the *mental state* of free harmony occasioned by the object is subjectively final. What makes such a mental state subjectively final, Allison suggests, is "not that we can grasp the explanation of its possibility only by deriving it from a will, but rather that it enhances the reciprocal activity of the imagination and understanding," and that it does this "in virtue of a structural feature of the state termed harmony or attunement, which is itself without purpose, since (in the state of free play) it does not aim at a determinate cognition" (*Kant's Theory of Taste: A Reading of the Critique of Aesthetic Judgment* [Cambridge: Cambridge University Press, 2001], 127).

8   CJ 5:187. Kant adds, however, that once we have incorporated a discovery into our ordinary experience, it no longer "arrests particular attention," and in order to take pleasure in it once again, we will need to bring its "heterogeneous" laws under "higher, though still always empirical, laws" (CJ 5:187).

9   It is plausible to take it that subjective finality is at the core of Kant's considered view on the source of the pleasure of beauty. As he puts it in the first introduction, "the representation of a subjective finality of an object is even identical with the feeling of pleasure" (FI 20:228). However, somewhat surprisingly, in the third *Critique*, Kant also toys with a different account of the source of the pleasure of beauty, claiming that it is bound up with our capacity to communicate with others. On such an account, the pleasure of beauty is nothing other than the pleasure that we feel in recognizing such a capacity. Thus, Kant claims in the Second Moment that when it comes to aesthetic judgment, the "universal capacity for being communicated incident to the mental state in the given representation" is fundamental, and only as a consequence of this capacity does there arise "the pleasure in the object" (CJ 5:217). Guyer identifies Kant's communicative account of beauty as an early view – but one that nonetheless has the capacity to continue to serve a useful role in aesthetic theory; see his "Pleasure and Society in Kant's Theory of Taste," in *Essays in Kant's Aesthetics*, ed. Paul Guyer and Ted Cohen (Chicago: University of Chicago Press, 1982), 87–114.

10   CJ 5:318.

11   CJ 5:445–446.

12   CJ 5:209.

13   CJ 5:207.

14   CJ 5:227.

15   Morals 6:452.

16   Morals 6:452–453.

17   Morals 6:402.

18   See also Christoph Horn's account of Kant's views on the place of love in the development of virtue, "The Concept of Love in Kant's Virtue Ethics," in *Kant's Ethics of Virtue*, ed. Monika Betzler (Berlin: Walter de Gruyter, 2008), 147–174.

19   Morals 6:455.

20   Morals 6:456.

21   Morals 6:456. Generally speaking, this describes the situation in which we feel gratitude as part of our experience of natural beauty. Since no human being has created the natural entity for which we feel grateful, there is no human being in particular who can receive our services in return. Our feelings of love may, consequently, be directed toward existing human beings, quite generally.

22   CPrR 5:76.

23   CPrR 5:83.

24   CPrR 5:83–84. Cf. *Religion*, where Kant equates "a heart joyous in the *compliance* with its duty (not just complacency in the *recognition* of it)" with virtue (Religion 6:23–24n).

25   Observations 2:217.

26   Of course, the *Observations* represents Kant's early ethical thought. In this work, he is roughly in agreement with moral sense theorists, including Shaftesbury and Hutcheson, that moral principles amount to "the consciousness of a feeling that lives in every human breast," as opposed to being "speculative rules" (Observations 2:217). He eventually came to reject his early approach. In lectures that he gave in 1785, he described moral sense views as those that seek to derive the "principle of morality from empirical grounds of inner experience" (Ethics 29:621): "[t]hose who assume a moral sense, whereby we are supposedly able, by feeling, to perceive the propriety or impropriety of our actions, have the principle of moral feeling. Shaftesbury introduced it, and had many Englishmen, including Hutcheson, among his followers" (Ethics 29:621).

In the *Groundwork* (also of 1785), Kant explicitly rejects such views: "*Empirical principles* are not at all fit to be the ground of moral laws. For, the universality with which these are to hold for all rational beings without distinction – the unconditional practical necessity which is thereby imposed upon them – comes to nothing if their ground is taken from the *special constitution of human nature* or the contingent circumstances in which it is placed" (Groundwork 4:442).

Even though Kant eventually rejected the moral theory that he had endorsed in the *Observations*, he did not also come to think that the notion of pathological love had no use. In fact, we see that he continues to invoke it in his moral psychology even in later works such as the *Metaphysics of Morals*.

27   Observations 2:217.

28   Observations 2:215.

29   Observations 2:216.
30   Observations 2:215–216.
31   Observations 2:216.
32   Observations 2:217.
33   Morals 6:382n.
34   CJ 5:267.

3

Beauty and Disinterestedness

Regardless of Whether the Object Exists or Not

In Section 59 of the third *Critique*, Kant writes that "[t]aste makes …
the transition from the charm of sense to habitual moral interest possible
without too violent a leap," and it does this to the extent that it "teaches
us to find, even in sensuous objects, a free delight apart from any charm
of sense."[1] There is a way, in other words, in which the pleasure of
beauty stands at a distance from the "habitual desires" that Kant refers
to as "inclinations," and this partly explains its capacity to contribute to
our moral development.

The idea that the pleasure of beauty is removed from our inclinations
in a way that the pleasure of agreeableness is not is a cornerstone of
Kantian aesthetics.[2] The pleasure of beauty is, as Kant puts it in the
Metaphysics of Morals, a contemplative pleasure, or a pleasure that is "not
connected with any desire for an object but is already connected with a
mere representation that one forms of an object (regardless of whether
the object of the representation exists or not)";[3] it is an "*inactive
delight*."[4] In the third *Critique*, he pursues this point by developing an
account of the "disinterestedness" of the pleasure of beauty.[5] In experiencing pleasure that stands at a distance from our desires, we feel as if we

The Possibility of Culture: Pleasure and Moral Development in Kant's Aesthetics,
First Edition. Bradley Murray.

are able to take a deep breath and to experience the world from a fresh, invigorating point of view. In this way, the experience of beauty is "directly attended with a feeling of the furtherance of life."[6] The pleasure of agreeableness, by contrast, does not stand at a distance from our desires. The pleasures of food and drink, tobacco, and so on, do not invite us to step back from our inclinations. If anything, they draw us further into our senses, and foster our existing tendency to become attached to objects that please us at this level.

In this chapter and the chapter that follows, we will begin by assuming that there is at least some plausibility to this general Kantian position on the disinterestedness of the pleasure of beauty. With this assumption in mind, the task will be to articulate a version of the position that makes sense of the experience of beauty – including artistic beauty – that many of us have. The underlying aim in doing so, of course, will be to consider how, given a broadly Kantian conception of the disinterestedness of the pleasure of beauty, the pursuit of this pleasure has the capacity to contribute to our moral development.

We saw a moment ago that Kant takes the distance from desire that characterizes the pleasure of beauty to consist partly in a kind of lack of concern regarding the existence of the object that we are finding beautiful. He claims, that is, that the pleasure concerns the representation of the object "regardless of whether the object of the representation exists or not." In the *Critique of Judgment*, too, Kant characterizes beauty's disinterestedness in similar terms. An interested pleasure, he claims, is one which is connected "with the representation of the existence of an object," and as such "always involves a reference to the faculty of desire."[7] A disinterested pleasure, by contrast, is one that is not essentially bound up with desire for the object, including the desire for it to exist. Moreover, in the First Moment, Kant writes:

> Now, where the question is whether something is beautiful, we do not want to know, whether we, or anyone else, are, or even could be, concerned in the real existence of the thing, but rather what estimate we form of it on mere contemplation (intuition or reflection). If anyone asks me whether I consider that the palace I see before me is beautiful, I may, perhaps, reply that I do not care for things of that sort that are merely made to be gaped at. Or I may reply in the same strain as that Iroquois *sachem* who said that nothing in Paris pleased him better than the eating-houses. I may even go

a step further and inveigh with the vigour of a *Rousseau* against the vanity of the great who spend the sweat of the people on such superfluous things. Or, in fine, I may quite easily persuade myself that if I found myself on an uninhabited island, without hope of ever again encountering human beings, and could conjure such a splendid edifice into existence by a mere wish, I should still not trouble to do so, so long as I had a hut there that was comfortable enough for me. All this may be admitted and approved; only it is not the point now at issue. All one wants to know is whether the mere representation of the object is to my liking, no matter how indifferent I may be to the real existence of the object of this representation. It is quite plain that in order to say that the object *is beautiful*, and to show that I have taste, everything turns on the meaning which I can give to this representation, and not on any factor which makes me dependent on the real existence of the object.[8]

There are, of course, reasons why, on one level, I might care about the "real existence" of the object that I find beautiful. For instance, if the object ceases to exist, so, too, does the pleasure I take in it. Insofar as I have a reason to pursue experiences of the pleasure of beauty – and, as I have been arguing, Kant's view is that we all have reason to do so as a means of pursuing moral development – then I also have reason to care about the existence of the object that I find beautiful. Moreover, if I am finding an artwork with historical significance to be beautiful, I may want it to continue to exist because I would not want to see the loss of an historical record. If I am finding a natural landscape to be beautiful, I may be concerned that there will be broader environmental repercussions if it ceases to exist.

However, on a plausible reading of passages such as the one just quoted, Kant's point is not that I must have no such concerns relating to the object's existence. Rather, his point is only that whatever desire I have for the object to exist is not central to the pleasure I feel.[9] My pleasure does not depend "on any factor which makes me dependent on the real existence of the object." It certainly does not derive from my possession or ownership of the object.[10] But even beyond the question of ownership or possession, there is a sense in which the pleasure is independent of the object's real existence. We can better see this if we contrast the pleasure of beauty with the pleasure of agreeableness. In the latter case, the object is considered insofar as it is capable of continuing to please *me*, so that the pleasure presupposes "the bearing [the object's] existence has upon my state so far as it is affected by such an object."[11] It is in this way that, central to the pleasure of agreeableness, is a "represented bond of connection between the Subject and the real existence of the object."[12] The pleasure of agreeableness is inexorably bound up with a representation of the object's continuing to exist for my selfish purposes. The pleasure of beauty, by contrast, is not.

Knowing What Sort of a Thing the Object is Intended to Be

Aside from the desire for an object to exist, there is a further desire that we may feel toward an object: the desire to understand it. Kant holds that part of what it means for the pleasure of beauty to be disinterested is that the latter desire cannot occupy a prominent place in experiences of this pleasure.

Thinkers influential to Kant had made this point. Burke, for example, suggested that "[i]t is not by the force of long attention and enquiry that we find any object to be beautiful," since "beauty demands no assistance from our reasoning."[13] There is certainly something to this line of thought. If the pleasure that I take in a poem derives primarily, say, from my intellectual understanding of why certain aspects of the poem make sense given what I know about the poet's biography, my pleasure is not one of beauty. For it is too bound up with my desire to achieve something intellectually, and in this sense the experience only reinforces more ordinary self-interested ways of experiencing the world. In a similar way, if the pleasure that I take in a wildflower in a meadow derives primarily from my successfully identifying the species to which it belongs as I work through a textbook on flowers, then my pleasure is not one of beauty.

Kant takes for granted such general points about the way in which the pleasure of beauty stands at a distance from our intellectual desires, and further refines them. He does this by exploring the complex relationship between the desire to understand what sort of thing the object is, that is, to understand its sortal classification, and the pleasure of beauty.

This issue is on Kant's mind partly because he wishes to address the question of how to draw the distinction between the pleasures of beauty and goodness. In a critique of taste, he writes, "it is of the utmost importance to decide whether beauty is really reducible to the concept of perfection."[14] The pleasure of perfection derives solely from an intellectual understanding of the object, and rationalist philosophers equate the pleasure of beauty with the pleasure of perfection.[15] In the end, Kant presents a nuanced position according to which conceptual understanding may play a limited role in the pleasure of beauty. But it is false to say that an experience of the pleasure of beauty may be based primarily on an intellectual understanding of the object, much less to say, as do the rationalists, that the pleasure is no different from the pleasure of perfection. In order to understand Kant's view on the connection between beauty and intellectual understanding, we will begin by considering his explanation as to what it takes to classify an object as belonging to a given sort. We will then consider his suggestion that, whereas the pleasure of "free beauty" is connected with a minimal degree of conceptual understanding of the object, the pleasure of "dependent beauty" may be connected with a higher degree of such understanding – while still differing in kind from the pleasure of perfection.

In an experience of the pleasure of goodness, we have seen, "the concept of an end is implied, and consequently the relation of reason to (at least possible) willing," so that "[t]o deem something good, I must always know what sort of a thing the object is intended to be, i.e. I must have a concept of it."[16] The pleasure of goodness, whether it takes the form of the pleasure of perfection or of utility, is a pleasure that only emerges in the context of our efforts to understand the object. Such efforts will partly involve making inferences as to the maker's intentions – to his or her "end" in acting. Kant uses the term "end" in two different, but related ways. He uses it to refer to a mental representation in the form of a *concept* that an agent employs in bringing an object into existence. Thus, he writes that the "concept of an Object, so far as it contains the ground of the actuality of this Object, is called its *end*."[17] Kant also uses the term "end" to refer to the very *object* that the agent brings into existence, insofar as its coming into existence is the effect of an action that was guided by the agent's end, in the concept sense. He uses the word in the object sense when he claims that "an end is the object of a concept so far as this concept is regarded as the cause of the object (the real ground of its possibility)."[18] Anything that is an end in the object sense is inseparable from an end in the concept sense.

Insofar as we are speaking of a maker's ends in acting, we are, in Kant's view, speaking of his or her "faculty of desire" and "will." The faculty of desire is a faculty which "*by means of its representations is the cause of the actuality of the objects of those representations.*"[19] The will, according to Kant, is "the faculty of desire, so far as it is determinable only through concepts, i.e. so as to act in conformity with the representation of an end."[20] Through acts of will, then, makers bring desired objects into existence.[21]

Kant's account brings out the way in which the maker's end plays a crucial role in settling the identity of the object that comes into existence. To see this, we can contrast two cases of making. In the first case, someone makes a cabin, say, by hammering together some wood with nails so that the structure has a suitable form. At some point, the process of making the cabin is complete: there is an object in the woods – the cabin – that is the product of the maker's labor. The maker's action has occurred in conformity with his conceptual representation – and this will at least partly include the sortal concept "cabin." In the second case, a different agent makes an object that is a physical duplicate of the cabin, but this maker had not set out to make a cabin at all. She does not even know what a cabin is. Instead, she was making a structure that was to be used in a religious ceremony. Its function is not that of a cabin (for example, providing shelter from the elements), but that of a religious symbol (for example, keeping a deity happy). Despite their physical similarity, these two objects are fundamentally different sorts of things. What explains this difference? The explanation is that one maker desired that a *cabin* should come into existence, and the other that a *religious symbol* should come into existence.

We can see that, when it comes to experiencing the pleasure of goodness, an intellectual process of interpreting the object, and in so doing, interpreting the maker's intentions, is crucial. We cannot experience this pleasure without first arriving at some understanding of what sort of object it is, and arriving at such an understanding, in turn, partly involves making certain inferences as to what it was intended by its maker to be. In order to experience the cabin as being good, I need to understand it to be a cabin and not a religious symbol, since the standards of goodness differ for objects of these two different kinds.

Keeping in mind the crucial role of the maker's desire not only in bringing the object into existence in the first place, but also in serving to ground the pleasure of goodness we may take in the object helps us to understand a remark that Kant makes in the Introduction to the *Metaphysics of Morals*. He claims that any pleasure that is connected with desire is a "practical" pleasure, and that practical pleasure can either be "the cause or the effect of the desire."[22] If a pleasure "necessarily precedes a desire" as its cause, he continues, then "the practical pleasure must be called an interest of inclination"; but if a pleasure "can only follow upon an antecedent determination of the faculty of desire it is an intellectual pleasure, and the interest in the object must be called an interest of reason."[23] The distinction between the case in which the pleasure is the cause of the desire and the case in which the desire is the cause of the pleasure corresponds to the distinction that Kant draws in the third *Critique* between the pleasures of agreeableness and goodness.[24] In the case of the pleasure of agreeableness, the pleasure is the cause of desire, in the sense that pathological pleasure has an addictive quality, leading us to desire more of the object causing the pleasure. But in the case of the pleasure of goodness, the desire precedes the pleasure in the following sense: the *thing* that is desired is the object in which we take the pleasure of goodness, and the relevant *person* who desires the object is, in the first instance, the object's maker. To say that the desire precedes the pleasure in the case of the pleasure of goodness is to bring out the way in which the pleasure is essentially grounded in an understanding of the nature of the maker's original desires in relation to the object.

Although Kant sometimes talks as if no experience involving any effort at understanding the object could count as an experience of the pleasure of beauty, this is not his final view. He talks in this way, for instance, when he writes that beauty "is wholly independent of the representation of the good," which "presupposes an objective purposiveness, i.e. the reference of the object to a determinate end."[25] Kant sometimes even talks as if the pleasure of beauty is an experience that might be free from conceptualization of any kind. Along these lines, he writes that "the delight in the manifold of a thing, in reference to the internal end that determines its possibility, is a delight based on a concept, whereas delight in the beautiful is such as does not presuppose any concept, but is immediately coupled with the representation through which the object is given (not through which it is thought)."[26]

Certainly the suggestion that the pleasure of beauty involves the application of *no* concept whatsoever seems too strong. This is at odds with Kant's own claim in the second edition of the *Critique of Pure Reason*, namely that all experience, including experience at the level of apprehension, requires the involvement of at least categorial concepts. He claims, that is, that "all synthesis, through which even perception itself becomes possible, stands under the categories, and since experience is cognition through connected perceptions, the categories are conditions of the possibility of experience."[27] If this is true, then it could not strictly speaking be correct to say that we apply absolutely no concepts while undergoing experiences of contemplative pleasure, much less any other experience.[28] Kant suggests a less extreme version of the "no concept" view when he writes that aesthetic pleasure lacks the involvement of any "concept for the purpose of a definite cognition."[29] An experience may properly be called one of beauty if there is conceptualization, just as long as the conceptualization is not for the purpose of a "definite cognition." It is not entirely clear, however, what Kant has in mind here by a "definite cognition." Is this the cognition of the object as falling under a basic sortal concept that determines the kind of thing it is? Is it perhaps the cognition of the object as falling under a higher-level sortal concept?[30]

Although these may be interesting questions as to how to interpret the specific passages in question, what can plausibly be thought of as Kant's "final" view on the question of the place of conceptualization in aesthetic pleasure shifts somewhat, and emerges most clearly in Section 16 of the third *Critique*. Even just prior to this section, Kant hints at the flexible position that he wishes to adopt, allowing that, in the case of perfection, we are dealing with "what is more akin to the predicate of beauty."[31] In Section 16, he writes:

> There are two kinds of beauty: free beauty (*pulchritudo vaga*), or beauty which is merely dependent (*pulchritudo adhaerens*). The first presupposes no concept of what the object should be; the second does presuppose such a concept and, with it, an answering perfection of the object. Those

of the first kind are said to be (self-subsisting) beauties of this thing or that thing; the other kind of beauty, being attached to a concept (conditioned beauty), is ascribed to objects which come under the concept of a particular end.[32]

The pleasure of free beauty does not derive from any sortal understanding of the object, whereas the pleasure of dependent beauty may partly derive from such an understanding. We might put Kant's position in the following way. Sometimes when we feel the pleasure of beauty – and especially when we feel this pleasure while engaging with artworks – our pleasure depends partly on knowing what sort of thing the object is. It can matter to my experience of a poem's beauty that I know that I am engaging with a poem and not a shopping list, that I know that it is a sonnet and not an epic, that I know that it is a poem about love, and so on. We might explain this by invoking the notion of subjective finality.[33] What is pleasurable about objects in which we take the pleasure of beauty is that they feel to us as if they were "pre-adapted" to, or designed to fit with, our cognitive capacities. But with certain objects – and particularly with human artifacts – a precondition of being able to experience them as pre-adapted to us will be that we know what sorts of things they are. Knowing that I am engaging with a poem and not a shopping list can make a difference when it comes to my capacity to experience it as subjectively final.

In the following chapter, we will see that this picture is supplemented by Kant's claim that we may carry out a special action, which he refers to as "abstraction," in order to experience the beauty of objects with "determinate internal ends." These are objects that seem to us to have been made. Kant's view is that we may become preoccupied with trying to understand such objects. Abstracting amounts to stepping back from the desire to understand in order to occupy a more disinterested position with respect to the object. Disinterestedness is best thought of as being a matter of degree. But this does not obviate the need to invoke the distinction between the pleasure of beauty and the pleasure of goodness. Even if it is true that some degree of understanding may be a precondition for experiencing certain aspects of an object's beauty, it is also true that experiences of the pleasure of goodness are characterized by conceptual understanding in a way and to a degree that experiences of beauty are not. In the case of beauty, our understanding of the object can at most contribute to our experience of its beauty, but cannot take centre stage.[34]

The Mere Representation of the Object

One way in which an aesthetic theory might develop the idea that the pleasure of beauty is disinterested is to invoke a special subjective object to which we attend while we are experiencing beauty, which stands in for the ordinary sensible object. On such a view, I am pleased, say, by my subjective representation of the wildflower rather than by the wildflower itself. Invoking a subjective object as the true object of my pleasure in experiences of beauty would, it is true, be a way of ensuring that I do not feel any desires toward an external object while I am experiencing the pleasure of beauty. However, reflection on the experience of beauty simply does not reveal it to have this character. I take my pleasure in the painting itself and in the wildflower itself – not merely in the impressions that these objects make in my visual field.

Commentators do not line up on whether to interpret Kant as endorsing this sort of "special object" view.[35] There does, however, seem to be at least some reason to think that Kant has such a view in mind, particularly when he speaks of the role of the "mere representation" and "mere apprehension" of the object. When it comes to beauty, he has claimed, the only relevant question is "whether the mere representation of the object is to my liking."[36] Beauty is not connected with any desire for an object but is instead "connected with a mere representation that one forms of an object (regardless of whether the object of the representation exists or not)."[37] In the Introduction to the third *Critique*, Kant expands on this idea, writing that "[i]f pleasure is connected with the mere apprehension (*apprehensio*) of the form of an object of intuition, apart from any reference it may have to a concept for the purpose of a definite cognition, this does not make the representation referable to the object, but solely to the subject."[38] Thus, on one way of reading these passages, Kant is suggesting that the pleasure of beauty results when we engage with a purely subjective representation of the object, rather than with the external object itself.

To better understand this possibility, it will help to have in mind Kant's theory of synthesis. In the *Critique of Pure Reason*'s first edition transcendental deduction, Kant claims that a mental process involving three stages must occur if we are to be capable of experiencing external objects. These stages are synthesis of apprehension, synthesis of reproduction, and synthesis of recognition in the concept.

Kant's view is that earlier stages are logically prior to later stages, which he takes to constitute progressively greater cognitive achievements. The stage of synthesis of apprehension gives rise to a kind of basic unity in the "manifold," that is, in the diverse collection of elements that make up our experience. At this stage the manifold is first "run through," and then its manifoldness is "taken together," with the result that its elements are "ordered, connected, and brought into relations."[39]

At the completion of the stage of synthesis of apprehension, we are left with an experience that does not represent whole, persisting objects located in space and time. For us to have this more robust kind of experience, Kant claims, syntheses of reproduction and of recognition in the concept must occur. Synthesis of reproduction appears to involve a kind of memory function which enables us to experience the manifold as having unity over time rather than merely at a given time, and synthesis of recognition in the concept enables us to go beyond this in order to be able to enjoy experiences of objects in the "weighty" sense of the term.[40] Kant reasons that it is only by positing the occurrence of synthesis of recognition in the concept that we are able to explain the necessity that is bound up with such experiences. As he puts it, "our thought of the relation of all cognition to its object carries something of necessity with it, since namely the latter is regarded as that which is opposed to our cognitions being determined at pleasure or arbitrarily rather than being determined *a priori*."[41] Insofar as our cognitions are to relate to an object, he holds, they "must also necessarily agree with each other in relation to it," which means that "they must have that unity that constitutes the concept of an object."[42]

Whether or not Kant's theory of synthesis turns out to be plausible as a general theory of object perception, it does at least suggest certain phenomenological claims concerning the ways in which we are able to attend to our experience. There is some reason to think, moreover, that Kant presupposes such claims in his account of the pleasure of beauty. Experiencing this pleasure while we are attending to an object at the level of apprehension would involve attending to the elements of our perception of the object as they present themselves in our moment-to-moment experience. In this way, we would not be attending to the external object as an object, as an object in the weighty sense. Thus, a natural way of reading Kant's claim that in an experience of the pleasure of beauty, the representation will not be "referable to the Object, but solely to the Subject" will be to take it to mean that we are attending primarily to the characteristics of the visual field. The experience will perhaps be similar to the kind of experience that painters sometimes describe when they are looking at an object that they are about to paint. For most of us, such an experience is not our everyday experience of the world – yet it does seem plausible to suggest that such an experience is at least possible.[43]

Supposing that there is a side of Kant that is inclined toward building the special object view into an account of the pleasure of beauty, the fact remains that the view fails to capture the phenomenology of the experience of beauty. Therefore, we have reason to exclude it from a fully developed account of the disinterestedness of aesthetic pleasure.

Sustine et Abstine

Whereas the pleasure of agreeableness draws us further into our senses and fosters our existing tendency to become attached to objects that give us enjoyment, the pleasure of beauty stands at a distance from our sensory desires. The pleasure of beauty is not radically disinterested – it is not a state characterized by the application of absolutely no concepts, and it is not a state in which we attend to a special subjective object. Rather, it is disinterested in the sense that our pleasure is not fundamentally bound up with desires we have toward the object with which we are engaging. Even if we begin with this relatively conservative conception of the disinterestedness of aesthetic pleasure, however, it is plausible to think that the pleasure of beauty makes a "transition from the charm of sense to habitual moral interest possible without too violent a leap."[44]

We learn through beauty what it is to step back from our inclinations.[45] On Kant's view, pursuing beauty will not be the only way of learning to distance ourselves from inclinations. In the *Lectures on Pedagogy*, for example, Kant suggests that in order to be capable of a "wise moderation" whereby the inclinations do not become passions, the preparation is "*sustine et abstine*."[46] He explains that the individual pursuing moral development must learn "to do without something when it is refused to him," and to "become accustomed to refusals, opposition, and so forth."[47] There is a way of practicing the discipline of the inclinations, then, that is quite arduous. Along these lines, in the *Anthropology*, Kant imagines a preacher involved in the moral education of a young person. Although the preacher will begin with a "cold instruction of the understanding" which simply invites reflection on the concept of duty – a kind of reflection of which this young person, as a rational agent, can be expected to be capable – the sermon proceeds to offer practical advice that will assist him in achieving his moral ends. The preacher offers the instruction: "Young man! Deny yourself gratifications (of amusement, indulgence, love, and so forth), if not with the Stoic intention of wanting to do without them completely, then with the refined Epicurean intention of having in view an ever-increasing enjoyment."[48]

Pursuing aesthetic pleasure enables us to learn to distance ourselves from our inclinations in a less arduous way – a way which we do not feel to be characterized by self-denial. For this reason, in pursuing culture by means of the pleasure of beauty, we succeed in making progress without having to take, as Kant puts it, "too violent a leap." It is true that the pupil in the case from the *Anthropology* may take solace in the expectation that he will one day enjoy the peace of mind that accompanies wisdom and moral virtue. But the fact remains that he is being asked to endure very unpleasant aspects of self-denial in the present in order to bring about this future wisdom. It is different with the pleasure of beauty. If the young person were to choose to pursue beauty, he would be pursuing his moral development in an enjoyable way. This difference speaks in favor of taking seriously the option of pursuing beauty as a means of pursuing culture.

There is a strain of the kind of anti-aesthetic thought that we considered in this book's introduction which finds ethical fault with beauty on the grounds that it is too removed from everyday life. We become lost in an inner world of disinterested pleasure, a mere "island of relief," and, as a consequence, neglect the social and political problems in the real world. However, from a Kantian point of view, as we have seen, part of the reason why we face the social and political problems we do is that, as individuals, we are not sufficiently morally developed. When we are deciding on courses of action, we do not extend our concern widely enough. We are too preoccupied with our inclinations. One way to change this would be to pursue experiences that cultivate in us the capacity to distance ourselves from such inclinations. From a Kantian point of view, then, the kind of anti-aesthetic thought under consideration does not properly recognize the transformative potential of the pleasure of beauty, which derives precisely from its distance from ordinary concerns.

Notes

1   CJ 5:354.
2   It is important to note that, on Kant's view, disinterestedness is in the first in-stance a feature of the *pleasure* one feels; see Nick Zangwill, "Unkantian Notions of Disinterest," *British Journal of Aesthetics* 32, no. 2 (1992): 149–152.
3   Morals 6:211.
4   Morals 6:212.
5   Until relatively recently, it was common for aesthetic theories to embrace the claim that the pleasure of beauty is disinterested. This changed partly because of George Dickie's influential attack on the notion of disinterested-ness, insofar as this constitutes a special action or mode of attention, in "The Myth of the Aesthetic Attitude," *American Philosophical Quarterly* 1 (1964): 56–65. Dickie's argument is partly phenomenological: "[w]hen the curtain goes up, when we walk up to a painting, or when we look at a sunset are we ever induced into a state of being distanced either by being struck by the beauty of the object or by pulling off an act of distancing?" He reports that he does not recall ever carrying out such "special actions" or being induced into such "special states" (56). The argument is also based partly on the premise that invoking a special mode of attention is theoretically unneces-sary to account for the relevant phenomena. Kant's view, of course, is in many ways at odds with Dickie's. However, it remains important to take seriously the Kantian view, since at the very least there is reason to question Dickie's characterization of the phenomenology of the experience of beauty. For a more general critique of Dickie's argument, see Jerome Stolnitz, "'The Aesthetic Attitude' in the Rise of Modern Aesthetics," *The Journal of Aes-thetics and Art Criticism* 36, no. 4 (1978): 409–422; and Gary Kemp, "The Aesthetic Attitude," *British Journal of Aesthetics* 39, no. 4 (1999): 392–399.
6   CJ 5:245.
7   CJ 5:205.
8   CJ 5:205.
9   See Henry Allison, *Kant's Theory of Taste: A Reading of the Critique of Aesthetic Judgment* (Cambridge: Cambridge University Press, 2001), 94–97. Kant takes pleasure to have what Rachel Zuckert describes as a formal structure of "future-directedness" (*Kant on Beauty and Biology* [Cambridge: Cambridge University Press, 2007], 231). This emerges in

the third *Critique*, where Kant defines pleasure as "[t]he consciousness of the causality of a representation in respect of the state of the subject as one tending *to preserve a continuance* of that state" (CJ 5:220). Pleasure, on this conception, is at least partly "about" its own continuation. Similarly, Kant writes in the first introduction: "Pleasure is a state of the mind in which a representation is in agreement with itself, as a ground, either merely for preserving this state itself (for the state of the powers of the mind reciprocally promoting each other in a representation preserves itself), or for producing its object. If it is the former, then the judgment on the given object is an aesthetic judgment of reflection; however, if it is the latter, then it is an aesthetic-pathological or an aesthetic-practical judgment" (FI 20:220).

If pleasure does indeed have such a structure, it might initially seem difficult to see how it could also be disinterested in the relevant sense. But, as Allison points out, we must distinguish between merely endeavoring to remain in a pleasurable mental state, and feeling an interested pleasure. The pleasure would be interested, Allison claims, "only if the endeavour were itself (at least partly) constitutive of the liking," which is not the case. Rather, "we endeavour to remain in a mental state because it is pleasurable; it is not pleasurable because we endeavour to remain in it" (97).

10 See Paul Guyer, *Kant and the Claims of Taste* (Cambridge: Cambridge University Press, 1997), 172. The view that the pleasure of beauty involves no desire to possess the object was common among Kant's contemporaries. Shaftesbury holds that it would be absurd to suggest that someone who required "the property or possession" of a tract of land in the country in order to enjoy it was truly finding it to be beautiful (*Characteristics of Men, Manners, Opinions, Times* [Cambridge: Cambridge University Press], 1999, 319). Edmund Burke holds that beauty involves love rather than lust: unlike love, lust is merely "an energy of the mind, that hurries us on to the possession of certain objects" (*A Philosophical Enquiry into the Origin of Our Ideas of the Sublime and Beautiful* [Oxford: Oxford University Press, 2008], 83). See also Stolnitz, "On the Origins of 'Aesthetic Disinterestedness,'" *Journal of Aesthetics and Art Criticism* 20, no. 2 (1961): 131–143.

11 CJ 5:207.

12 CJ 5:209.

13 Burke, *A Philosophical Enquiry*, 84. See also Francis Hutcheson, *An Inquiry into the Original of Our Ideas of Beauty and Virtue in Two Treatises* (Indianapolis: Liberty Fund, 2008), 24. See Stolnitz, "On the Origins of 'Aesthetic Disinterestedness,'" 134.

14 CJ 5:227.

15 Leibniz claims, for example, that "[p]leasure is the feeling of a perfection or an excellence," and holds that the pleasure of beauty is no exception

(Gottfried Wilhelm Leibniz, *Philosophical Papers and Letters: A Selection*, ed. Leroy E. Loemker [Dordrecht: Springer, 1989], 425). Christian Wolff writes that "[b]eauty consists in the perfection of things insofar as they are apt by the power in them to produce pleasure in us" (*Psychologia Empirica*, ed. Jean École [Hildesheim: Georg Olms, 1968], 420, §544), translation quoted from Frederick C. Beiser, *Diotima's Children* (Oxford: Oxford University Press, 2009), 63. And Moses Mendelssohn writes: "Everything capable of being represented to the senses as a perfection could also present an object of beauty. Belonging here are all the perfections of external forms, that is, the lines, surfaces, and bodies and their movements and changes; the harmony of the multiple sounds and colors; the order in the parts of a whole, their similarity, variety, and harmony; their transposition and transformation into other forms; all the capabilities of our soul, all the skills of our body. Even the perfections of our external state (under which honor, comfort, and riches are to be understood) cannot be excepted from this if they are fit to be represented in a way that is apparent to the senses" (*Moses Mendelssohn: Philosophical Writings*, ed. Daniel O. Dahlstrom [Cambridge University Press, 1997], 172).

For more on the German rationalist tradition in aesthetics, see Beiser, *Diotima's Children*.

16 CJ 5:207.

17 CJ 5:180.

18 CJ 5:220.

19 CJ 5:178n. See also the *Critique of Practical Reason*, where Kant describes the faculty of desire as "a being's faculty to be by means of its representations the cause of the reality of the objects of these representations" (CPrR 5:9–10n).

20 CJ 5:220.

21 In the "Analytic of Teleological Judgment," Kant invokes specific terminology to describe the nature of the causal connections involved when things come into existence. Specifically, he distinguishes between a "regressive" and "progressive" causal series. The former is a series of causes and effects in which one or more of the effects is an end, in the object sense. What makes such a series regressive is that the effect is in some way *prior* to its own cause. This is not, of course, to say that the effect literally precedes the cause in time. Instead, the effect is prior to the cause in the sense of being conceived of before its cause is initiated. For example, Kant claims, if someone builds a house in order to generate rent money, the representation of the effect – the house's existing and generating rent money – is at least partly the cause of the house's coming into existence. A progressive causal, by contrast, is a series of causes that progress toward the effect in

such a way that the effect is not prior to the causes, in the relevant sense. For example, there may be a series of events in which a gust of wind causes a rock to fall off a cliff and to strike another rock, causing the second rock to break apart. This is a merely progressive causal series insofar as the first rock's falling off the cliff is part of the explanation of the second rock's breaking, but the second rock's breaking is not part of the explanation of why the first rock falls off the cliff. Kant appears to take certain causal series, including the series that occurs in the case of the house built in order to generate rent money, to be both regressive and progressive. Thus, while it is true that the effect of the house's existing and generating rent money is at least partly the cause of the house's coming into existence, it is also true that the house's coming into existence is the cause of the rental income (CJ 5:372). Generally speaking, acts of making will involve regressive causal series, since makers typically conceive of the objects they make before they bring them into existence.

22   Morals 6:212.

23   Morals 6:212–213.

24   Kant also invokes the distinction between practical and non-practical pleasures in the third *Critique*: the pleasure of beauty, he writes, is "in no way practical, neither resembling that from the pathological ground of agreeableness nor that from the intellectual ground of the represented good" (CJ 5:222). Cf. FI 20:220.

25   CJ 5:226.

26   CJ 5:230. See also Section 15 of the third *Critique*, where Kant claims that it is precisely because "no concept," including "one of a definite end," figures into the "subjective grounds" on which a judgment of taste is based that beauty "involves no thought whatsoever of a perfection of the object" (CJ 5:228).

27   CPR B161.

28   Commentators have devoted a good deal of attention to the ambiguity inherent in Kant's presentation of his views on experience. Kant sometimes speaks as if there can be uncategorized experiences, yet at other times, he denies this possibility. The potential difficulty is that, if Kant does maintain that an application of the categories is required for any experience at all, and moreover that the application of the categories always yields an experience of objects in the weighty sense, then it is not clear how he will be in a position to account for experiences which are not experiences of such objects – including experiences that we have while dreaming. For more on this issue, see, e.g., Lewis White Beck, "Did the Sage of Königsberg Have No Dreams?," in *Essays on Kant and Hume* (New Haven: Yale University Press, 1978).

29   CJ 5:189.

30   For example, on David Wiggins's account of sortal concepthood, a sortal concept – such as "man" or "horse" – is a basic concept that gives an answer to the question "what is *x*?" asked of particular *x*s that lie in that concept's extension. The most fundamental sortal concepts are "substance sortal concepts." They provide the most general and informative answers to the aforementioned question, they apply to the entity at all times at which it exists, and they determine a principle of activity (for natural things) or function (for artifacts) corresponding to entities falling under their extensions. Phased sortals such as "cabinet minister," by contrast, are higher-level concepts that do not characterize the entity in this fundamental way, and need not apply to the entity throughout its entire life. See Wiggins, *Sameness and Substance Renewed* (Cambridge: Cambridge University Press, 2001).

31   CJ 5:227.

32   CJ 5:229.

33   See Chapter 2.

34   Along these lines, Guyer proposes that, although the experience of dependent beauty involves concepts of purpose, those concepts do not fully determine our approval of their objects. See Guyer, *Kant and the Claims of Taste*, 219. For a contrasting view, see Ruth Lorand, "Free and Dependent Beauty: A Puzzling Issue," *British Journal of Aesthetics* 29 (1989): 32–40. Lorand focuses on some of Kant's strong – and I would suggest misleading – remarks about the absence of conceptualization in experiences of beauty, and denies the very coherence of his distinction between free and dependent beauty.

35   Theodore Uehling, e.g., claims that "in an aesthetic judgment, the categories are in no sense 'applied' to the synthesized manifold of sensations," and consequently "there is no question of knowledge [or] cognition of the object represented by the organized synthesis in imagination" (*The Notion of Form in Kant's "Critique of Aesthetic Judgement"* [The Hague: Mouton, 1971]). On the other hand, many commentators – including Guyer – seek to avoid ascribing to Kant the view that experiences of beauty involve a special object of attention. Thus, Guyer claims that it would be "problematic" if Kant's view did not entail that the experience of beauty depended on "the perception of an actual empirical object" (*Kant and the Claims of Taste*, 177).

36   CJ 5:205.

37   Morals 6:211.

38   CJ 5:189.

39   CPR A99.

40   Kant explains that synthesis of reproduction must occur, since "[w]ithout consciousness that that which we think is the very same as what we thought a moment before, all reproduction in the series of representations would be in vain"; instead, it would be "a new representation in our current state, which would not belong at all to the act through which it had been gradually generated, and its manifold would never constitute a whole, since it would lack the unity that only consciousness can obtain for it" (CPR A103).

41   CPR A104.

42   CPR A104–105.

43   An even more extreme conception of such an account of aesthetic perception would incorporate the formalist view that Kant at times endorses, according to which it is our experience of merely formal elements that grounds our pleasure in an experience of beauty. That is, it is the experience of the object "in respect of its form as present in *apprehension* (*apprehensio*) prior to any concept" that grounds the pleasure (CJ 5:192). The principal notion of form that we find in the third *Critique* is that of spatiotemporal form, which Kant explains in terms of the notions of "figure" and "play" (CJ 5:225). The notion of figure applies most clearly in the case of visual form, and consists in the object's experienced lineal qualities (see Guyer, *Kant and the Claims of Taste*, 201). The notion of play applies to such things as auditory events, and consists in the relations between sound elements as they unfold in time. If we were to add the doctrine of formalism to the "special object" account, we would arrive at the view that, while we are experiencing beauty, insofar as we are already attending to the subjective qualities of our experience, our attention will be focused even more narrowly on form. Here, the form in question will not be the form of the object prompting our experience of pleasure as such, since we would not be representing the object as such to begin with. Attending to form under such circumstances might involve, in the visual case, attending to the lineal qualities present in our visual field at a given time. And, in the auditory case, it would perhaps involve attending to the relations among the elements in our subjective auditory experience, as it unfolds over time. But it is important to note that it is hardly obvious that there would be any very useful relation between these elements of our immediate experience and the spatiotemporal form of the objects themselves. For instance, simply viewing an object from a different angle can radically change the lineal qualities that are present to us in our visual fields. For more on Kant's notion of form, see Guyer, *Kant and the Claims of Taste*, ch. 6, and Uehling, *The Notion of Form in Kant's "Critique of Aesthetic Judgement."*

44   CJ 5:354.

45 Cf. Allison, *Kant's Theory of Taste*, 265.
46 Pedagogy 9:486. Cf. Ethics 27:392, Groundwork 4:428, and Ground-
    work 4:454.
47 Pedagogy 9:487.
48 Anthropology 7:165.

4

Art, Genius, and Abstraction

A Beautiful Soul – to Which No Connoisseur or Art Collector Can Lay Claim

When it comes to beauty, Iris Murdoch has suggested, our experience of art is more easily degraded than our experience of nature, since artistic experience is more likely to be a matter of "selfish obsession."[1] Consequently, our engagement with art is less capable of contributing to what she describes as a process of "unselfing" than is our engagement with nature. Kant certainly would have found himself at least somewhat sympathetic to such a point. In Kantian terminology, there is a question whether it is possible for our engagement with artworks to be sufficiently distanced from our desires in order for our pleasure to amount to one of beauty. This, in turn, raises a question whether our engagement with art can promote our culture by enabling a "transition from the charm of sense to habitual moral interest."[2] If it cannot, then we have reason to prefer nature over art insofar as we seek to develop morally.

Why, though, might there be a question as to our capacity to engage disinterestedly with art? One reason, which Rousseau articulated and to which Kant responds, is that the artworld can seem to foster morally problematic attitudes including vanity and an overconcern with our

The Possibility of Culture: Pleasure and Moral Development in Kant's Aesthetics,
First Edition. Bradley Murray.
© 2015 John Wiley & Sons, Inc. Published 2015 by John Wiley & Sons, Inc.

status and reputation. Artworks are treated as commodities that are bought and sold by museums and collectors, and in the process concerns over reputation can easily come to overshadow the appreciation of the works themselves. Moreover, it is possible that in engaging with a given artwork my pleasure will be bound up with thoughts about how others will view my appreciation of it – that it will be bound up, for instance, with the thought that others will view me as a person of taste. A second reason why there might be a question as to our capacity for disinterested engagement with art has to do with the fact that artworks are artifacts. There is, in Kant's view, a distinctive phenomenology of artifacts: these objects appear to us to have been made, and may, for this reason, mobilize in us a strong desire to understand them. Our desire to know "what sort of a thing the object is intended to be" may become all-consuming. Whereas it is possible to be pleased by an object's goodness if we are primarily concerned to understand it, it is not, as we have seen, possible to be pleased by its beauty if this is our primary concern. In what follows, we will consider, in turn, Kant's approach to these two concerns.

As far as the first concern goes, it is helpful to begin once again with Rousseau, whose attack on the arts in the *Discourse on the Sciences and the Arts* centered partly around his claim that the arts breed an excessive, self-centered concern with our reputations, which manifests itself partly in the vices of vanity and inauthenticity. According to Rousseau, "[b]efore Art had fashioned our manners and taught our passions to speak in ready-made terms, our morals were rustic but natural; and differences in conduct conveyed differences of character at first glance."[3] The inauthenticity that prevails as the arts thrive in a given society serves to cloud human relations, so that, even with one's friends, one will "have to wait for great occasions, that is, to wait until it is too late" to know their true characters.[4] By contrast, where human life is not corrupted in this way, Rousseau claims, our morals are allowed to be "rustic but natural," and it is simpler to know what those around us truly think.[5]

In Section 42 of the third *Critique*, Kant signals that he agrees with Rousseau that there are "*virtuosi* in matters of taste," who are "as a general rule, vain, capricious, and addicted to injurious passions."[6] Kant grants, moreover, that there is a sense in which it is better not to fuel our tendencies to feel such passions. For instance, he considers the case of an individual "with taste enough to judge of works of fine art with the greatest correctness" who is in a room containing artworks. If, Kant suggests, this person "readily quits the room in which he meets with those beauties that minister to vanity or, at least, social joys, and betakes himself to the beautiful in nature, so that he may there find as it were a feast for his spirit in a train of thought which he can never completely evolve, we will then regard this choice even with veneration, and give him credit for a beautiful soul." Such a soul is something to which "no connoisseur or art collector can lay claim."[7] In Kant's view, this person is to be venerated for coming to recognize that his pleasure in the artworks is bound up with vanity and his interest in his social life, and for choosing as a consequence to devote himself to the appreciation of natural beauty.

When we are preoccupied with a concern with our reputations as we pursue the arts, our pleasure is not characterized by disinterestedness. This is not to say that there is no possibility of being pleased disinterestedly by art. It is only to say that our artistic practices generate obstacles to disinterested engagement, and that those who pursue the arts in a way that is characterized by the problematic attitudes in question will not develop morally in virtue of experiencing a disinterested pleasure.

However, even when it comes to the moral implications of the practices of the "*virtuosi* of taste," Kant's view is more subtle than it might first appear. For he holds that there is a way in which the very practices that hinder their ability to engage disinterestedly with the arts can contribute to their moral development. There is a sense, Kant believes, in which Rousseau is mistaken to object to our maintaining a concern for reputation, vanity, and manners – including when we do so as part of our engagement with artworks. It is true, of course, that there is a difference between merely having good manners and actually being virtuous. In the First Moment of the *Critique of Judgment*, for instance, Kant claims that "there may be correct habits (conduct) without virtue, politeness without good-will, propriety without honour, &c."[8] Similarly, he claims in the *Anthropology* that making someone well-mannered is not the same as "forming him into a morally good person." And yet, being well-mannered is not morally insignificant. For this includes, Kant claims, not only "the appearance or demeanour of moral goodness," but also a degree of moral goodness itself – and this is because being well-mannered indicates that we have the inclination to "place a value even on the semblance of moral goodness."[9] We may, for instance, put another's needs before our own in a given situation without understanding that doing so is morally required, but only because we care to cultivate a good reputation in the eyes of others. While it is true that in doing so we are not fully virtuous, it is still praiseworthy that we have at least managed to do this much. As we have seen, Kant's view is that practicing carrying out actions that conform with duty helps us to develop as moral agents in the long run, even if the motivation underlying such actions contains self-interest. The social graces of affability, etiquette, and tolerance, Kant claims in the *Metaphysics of Morals*, "make virtue fashionable" by serving to "promote the feeling for virtue itself by a striving to bring this illusion as near as possible to the truth."[10]

Of course, the art connoisseur who is caught up with his status and reputation in his dealings with art is not necessarily seeking a reputation as a virtuous person, specifically. But the general spirit of Kant's previously mentioned points applies nonetheless. Beneath this person's vain concerns, Kant suggests, lies a deep concern for communicating with others, in a broad sense of "communication," where this has fundamentally to do with our capacity to relate to other human beings. One reason why we might be concerned with how we are viewed aesthetically in the eyes of others – and one reason why we might engage in related posturing with regard to our aesthetic taste – is precisely that we ultimately care that we will be able to relate to these others. We care whether we will have a source of pleasure in common, and this concern is morally significant.[11] This seems to be the point to which Kant is gesturing in his discussion of the "empirical interest in the beautiful" in Section 41 of the third *Critique*. Such an interest, Kant claims, "exists only in *society*," a point which he seeks to illustrate using the example of an isolated individual:

> With no one to take into account but himself a man abandoned on a desert island would not adorn either himself or his hut, nor would he look for flowers, and still less plant them, with the object of providing himself with personal adornments. Only in society does it occur to him to be not merely a man, but a man refined after the manner of his kind (the beginning of a civilization) – for that is the estimate formed of one who has the bent and turn for communicating his pleasure to others, and who is not quite satisfied with an object unless his feeling of delight in it can be shared in communion with others.[12]

Those who pursue artworks in social contexts and who do so in ways that are characterized by a self-conscious concern with the ways in which they will be viewed in the eyes of others will, in at least some cases, betray at the same time a laudable aspiration: namely, to be accepted as part of a community grounded in commonalities of taste. The community in question is perhaps merely an idealization rather than an actually existing one. Yet such an aspiration is noteworthy precisely because the capacity to experience pleasures of taste transcends many of the ways in which we typically divide our communities. It is morally significant in the long run because developing morally requires that we become better able to expand our concern beyond ourselves, and even beyond those who are close to us. Only a universal concern for humanity can underpin genuine virtue, and Kant holds out hope that social practices that are common in the artworld – even if they fall short of being virtuous in themselves – can play some role in helping us to expand our sense of community. Keeping this in mind can shed light on Kant's description, in the *Idea for a Universal History*, of humankind's awakening as taking place by means of steps "from crudity toward culture."[13] He envisions the third and final step of this developmental process as one in which there is a transformation of "a pathologically compelled agreement" to form a society "into a *moral* whole," but just prior to this, he believes, lies an all-important second step – namely, the step in which "taste is formed."[14]

A Contingency of Form

Those who pursue the arts in ways that are bound up with vanity and a concern with their reputations may develop morally as a result, but the cause of such development is not that their pleasure in the arts is characterized by disinterestedness. Of course, it is not inevitable that we must be preoccupied with vanity and reputation as we pursue the arts. Insofar as we are not, it seems, the door remains open for us to be pleased disinterestedly by the artworks with which we engage. However, Kant foresees another potential obstacle to disinterestedness. As mentioned above, this obstacle is that, since artworks are artifacts, they have a distinctive phenomenology which can mobilize in us a strong desire to understand them.

When we reflect on our experience of artifacts, we notice that they typically present themselves as artifacts, rather than, say, as natural objects. In the Analytic of Teleological Judgment, Kant draws our attention to this phenomenon by considering what it would be like for us to come across a hexagonally-shaped figure in the sand:

> Suppose a person was in a country that seemed to be uninhabited and was to see a geometrical figure, say a regular hexagon, traced on the sand. As he reflected, and tried to form a concept of the figure, his reason would make him conscious, though perhaps obscurely, that in the production of this concept there was unity of principle. His reason would then forbid him to consider the sand, the neighbouring sea, the winds, or even animals with their footprints, as causes familiar to him, or any other irrational cause, as the ground of the possibility of such a form. For the contingency of coincidence with a concept like this, which is only possible in reason, would appear to him so infinitely great that there might just as well be no law of nature at all in the case. Hence, it would seem that the cause of the production of such an effect could not be contained in the mere mechanical operation of nature, but that, on the contrary, a concept of such an object, as a concept that only reason can give and compare the object with, must likewise be what alone contains that causality. On these grounds it would appear to him that this effect was one that might without reservation be regarded as an end, though not as a natural end. In other words he would regard it as a product of *art – vestigium hominis video*.[15]

In viewing the hexagon in the sand, our conscious experience would represent what we see as a designed object. It would be difficult to accept that solely "natural" events – events involving, say, the movement of the wind or the sea – could be the ground of the possibility of an object with just such a form.[16] The coincidence of such events occurring together in just the way needed to bring the hexagon into existence would appear "infinitely great." As a consequence we would inevitably experience the figure as having been brought into existence by a maker. The figure is an "end" (in the object sense) that was brought into existence by a maker who had an "end" (in the concept sense) in act-ing.[17] This makes the figure a "product of art," or in other words, an artifact.[18]

Of course, there are no necessary connections between the form an object has and its causal history.[19] It is always possible that an object with a form that seems as if it could only have come into existence through an act of making actually originated by means of a purely natural pro-cess. It is at least *remotely* possible that the wind should have caused just such a hexagonal figure to occur in the sand. It is equally possible that someone should design an object to seem undesigned, so that it looks like a natural object. For example, an object crafted to look just like a small rock found in nature could be too realistic for anybody to be able to tell, on the basis of observing its outer features alone, that it is artifactual. At most, we can say that there are certain appearances that objects can have that are suggestive of design or lack of design. And Kant seems to recognize this point, which is precisely why he speaks here in terms of the unlikelihood, rather than the strict impossibility, of the hexagon's having come into existence without design.

In any case, generally speaking, our experiences of artifacts tend to incorporate representations of the objects *as* artifacts. When we see a house, a lamp, or a book, we experience the object in question as having been made by someone with a specific end in acting. Of course, this point applies to artifacts which are artworks. We experience paintings, sculptures, works of architecture and music, and so on, as things that have been brought into existence through design. This feature of our experience of artifacts has implications, on Kant's view, when it comes to the experience of beauty. When we recognize an object to be an artifact, we tend to interpret it and try to understand it. Recall the two cases of making, considered earlier, which yield objects that are physical duplicates, but which fall under very different sortal concepts. In the first case, someone makes an object that is supposed to be a cabin. The act of making occurs in a way that is guided by the sortal concept "cabin." In the second case, someone makes an object that is a physical duplicate of the cabin without setting out to make a cabin at all, and without even knowing what a cabin is. Her intention is to make a symbol that is to be used in a religious ceremony. Despite their physical similarity, these two objects are fundamentally different sorts of things. The explanation of the difference between them is that one maker desired that a *cabin* should come into existence, and the other that a *religious symbol* should come into existence. It is possible to interpret these physically indiscernible artifacts in these very different ways, and we find that we have an interest in knowing what sort of thing the object is supposed to be.

Kant's view, as we saw in the previous chapter, is that although the desire to understand can coexist with the pleasure of beauty, in the form of dependent beauty, the pleasure remains a disinterested one only to the extent that this desire does not occupy a prominent place. Because artifacts present themselves to us as intentionally made, there will be a tendency for our desire to understand to predominate. Thus, there is a question as to what it might take to overcome our tendency to engage with artifacts, including artworks, in a way that is dominated by a desire for understanding. And it is necessary to address this question if we are fully to explain how it is possible to be pleased disinterestedly by artworks.

We are "not always obliged," Kant writes, "to look with the eye of reason into what we observe (i.e. to consider it in its possibility)." For even when we observe a "finality with respect to form, and trace it in objects," we need not do so while also "resting it on an end (as the material of the *nexus finalis*)."[20] It is possible, in other words, to step back from our desire to understand objects that seem to have been made. Although there is a sense in which the existence of an object such as the hexagon in the sand is only "explicable and intelligible for us by virtue of an assumption on our part of a fundamental causality according to ends," there is also a sense in which we can put aside questions we have about the possibility of its existence and engage with it in a way that is characterized by disinterestedness.

Kant uses the term "finality" (*Zweckmäßigkeit*) here to refer to a feature that an object may possess, namely, that of seeming to be related to a maker's concept, "so far as this concept is regarded as the cause of the object (the real ground of its possibility)."[21] To possess finality is to possess the property of seeming to have come into existence through an act of making. It is important for Kant to invoke the general notion of finality, since the points he wishes to make are not limited to artifacts, but also apply to some natural objects. That is, both artifacts and natural objects may possess finality, according to Kant. This will become clearer once we consider his examples of abstraction.[22]

Kant explicitly takes up the topic of abstraction in Section 16 of the third *Critique*. He writes: "[i]n respect of an object with a determinate internal end, a judgement of taste would only be pure where the person judging either has no concept of this end, or else makes abstraction from it in his judgement."[23] An object with a "determinate internal end" is simply one that possesses finality. It is possible, Kant is claiming, for us to make a pure judgment of taste – that is, one grounded in a disinterested pleasure – insofar as we do not for some reason recognize the object as possessing finality, or, if we do recognize it, insofar as we carry out an act of abstraction. Doing the latter amounts to not looking "with the eye of reason into what we observe." Let us consider some of Kant's examples. On the one hand, we can experience the bright spots in the night sky as "suns moving in orbits prescribed for them with the wisest regard to ends." But, on the other hand, we can also experience the night sky while abstracting from such thoughts, which would mean experiencing it "just as it strikes the eye, as a broad and all-embracing canopy." We can experience the oceans as "mighty reservoirs from which are drawn the vapours that fill the air with clouds of moisture for the good of the land," or we can abstract in order to experience them "as the poets do, according to what the impression upon the eye reveals," namely as nothing but a "clear mirror of water bounded only by the heavens."[24] We can experience a flower as the botanist does in the course of his or her work, by employing a theory that invokes teleological notions which make reference to the flower's nature and purpose. But we – and even the botanist – can pay "no attention to this natural end" in order to be pleased by the flower's beauty.[25]

These examples concern natural phenomena rather than artifacts, which may seem peculiar. The contrast with which we began was one between artifacts, which seem to have a designed quality, and natural phenomena, which do not. However, from Kant's point of view, this is an oversimplification. For we do sometimes experience natural phenomena as if they had been designed. As will emerge more clearly in Chapter 6, Kant's view is that we adopt such an as-if stance when we are pursuing teleological explanations of nature – including when we are working scientifically. This is why Kant suggests that the botanist needs to abstract in order to experience the flower as beautiful. The botanist can be expected, because of his or her profession, to have developed a tendency to experience the flower as if it had been designed, since adopting this perspective grounds the relevant teleological explanations. The botanist will need to set aside this desire to understand the flower, ceasing to think of it as designed, in order to be in a position to be pleased disinterestedly while engaging with it. Even though Kant's examples do not centre on artifacts, he is clearly taking for granted that we will need to abstract if we are to be pleased disinterestedly by them. In fact, on a plausible understanding of his account of artistic genius, which we will consider shortly, it turns out partly to be an account of what it is like for us to abstract in our engagement with artworks.

Abstracting, then, is a way of attending to the object as it "strikes the eye," or "as the poets do." It involves taking a step back in our experience of the object so that this experience is not taken over by our desire to understand the object. Even though it is right to say that abstraction is needed in order to experience the pleasure of beauty while engaging with objects manifesting finality, such as the hexagon in the sand, it is also right to maintain the flexible position considered in the previous chapter concerning the relationship between the pleasures of beauty and understanding. The pleasure of beauty can be partly grounded in knowing what sort of thing an object is. As already mentioned, it matters to the experience of a poem's beauty that I am recognizing it to be a poem, a sonnet, a love poem, and so on. We can acknowledge this while still recognizing that experiences of the pleasure of goodness are bound up with understanding in a way that experiences of beauty are not. When I am experiencing the pleasure of beauty while engaging with a poem, my attempts at understanding it do not predominate my experience. If my pleasure is highly bound up with my desire to understand it, I must abstract if I wish to experience the work's beauty. Given that disinterestedness is a matter of degree, the more I am able to abstract, the closer my pleasure comes to being one of free beauty.

Through Which Nature Gives the Rule to Art

So far, we have considered Kant's account of making insofar as it describes standard cases – those in which the maker forms very determinate representations relating to the identity of what is being made, and also forms a plan as to how to bring it into existence. But what if there were a way of making an object that did not involve the maker's forming such determinate representations? This, arguably, is just what making something by employing the productive capacity that Kant refers to as "genius" would amount to. The sense in which making something through genius is not guided by determinate representations of the object becomes clearer once we consider two features of genius, on Kant's account: first, those who make artworks through genius do not operate on the basis of a conscious "rule" governing the act of making; and second, those who make works in this way lack insight into how, specifically, they have brought the artwork into being.

In the first place, Kant describes genius as a "*talent* for producing that for which no definite rule can be given: and not an aptitude in the way of cleverness for what can be learned according to some rule."[26] In making something by relying on this talent, the maker is not consciously following a set of rules or a plan. Instead, he or she is guided by what is more akin to moment-to-moment inspiration – the maker will, as it were, let himself or herself go in the process. Kant comments on the origins of the word "genius," emphasizing its connection with the idea of carrying out work guided by inspiration: it originally refers to the "peculiar guardian and guiding spirit bestowed upon a human being at birth, by the inspiration of which those original ideas were obtained."[27]

Second, Kant claims, genius "cannot indicate scientifically how it brings about its product, but rather gives the rule as *nature*," so that "where an author owes a product to his genius, he does not himself know how the *ideas* for it have entered into his head, nor has he it in his power to invent the like at pleasure, or methodically, and communicate the same to others in such precepts as would enable them to produce similar products."[28] For example, Kant suggests, "no *Homer* or *Wieland* can show how his ideas, so rich at once in fancy and in thought, enter and assemble themselves in his brain, for the good reason that he does not himself know, and so cannot teach others."[29] Kant's underlying point is that in producing an object through genius, the maker lacks self-knowledge, in the sense of being unaware of how the process proceeds as it does.[30]

It can seem at times as if Kant holds that the *only* way in which an artist might make a beautiful artwork is by doing so through genius. In Section 46 of the third *Critique*, he claims, for instance, that "fine art is only possible as a product of genius":

> For every art presupposes rules which are laid down as the foundation which first enables a product, if it is to be called one of art, to be represented as possible. The concept of fine art, however, does not permit of the judgement upon the beauty of its product being derived from any rule that has a *concept* for its determining ground, and that depends, consequently, on a concept of the way in which the product is possible. Consequently fine art cannot of its own self excogitate the rule according to which it is to realize its product. But since, for all that, a product can never be called art unless there is a preceding rule, it follows that nature in the individual (and by virtue of the harmony of his faculties) must give the rule to art, i.e. fine art is only possible as a product of genius.[31]

One reading of this passage – which can be called the "metaphysical reading" – takes it that Kant is seeking to establish that any artwork that we may experience as beautiful must, *in fact,* have been produced through the maker's productive capacity of genius.[32] However, the trouble with such a reading is that it posits a very strong connection between the way in which an object comes into existence and the kind of pleasure we may take in it.[33] But an object that we experience as beautiful may have been brought into existence in various ways. We can even imagine a case in which an artwork that we find beautiful is a copy of another work. But copying, of course, does not require exercising genius.[34]

If the metaphysical reading lacks plausibility, there remains a second, more promising, reading. On this reading – which can be called the "epistemological reading" – we take it that Kant's doctrine of genius is to function partly as an extension of his account of abstraction. To say that I am experiencing an artwork as having been produced through genius is a way of saying that I am abstracting. In not looking "with the eye of reason" into what I observe, and thereby putting aside my thoughts concerning the object's having a "determinate internal end," I am experiencing the artwork as if it were the product of mere nature, rather than as the product of a determinate act of making. Along these lines, Kant emphasizes the connection between the concept of genius and the concept of a natural process. He writes that the concept of genius is the concept of "nature in the individual," that genius "is the talent (natural endowment) which gives the rule to art," and that since talent, "as an innate productive faculty of the artist, belongs itself to nature, we may put it this way: *Genius* is the innate mental aptitude (*ingenium*) *through which* nature gives the rule to art."[35]

The epistemological reading helps us to make sense of some of Kant's remarks about artistic beauty that might otherwise seem quite surprising. He says, for example, that a beautiful artwork will have "the appearance of nature," that "the finality in its form must appear just as free from the constraint of arbitrary rules as if it were a product of mere nature,"[36] that it must not "have the appearance of being intentional," and that it must be "clothed with the aspect of nature."[37] We might initially be tempted to think that Kant is suggesting, implausibly, that when we encounter beautiful artworks, we will literally mistake them for natural objects. However, if we have in mind the epistemological reading, we may instead understand Kant to be making a point about the phenomenology of abstraction in cases involving artworks. When we abstract in order to experience an artwork as beautiful, we will experience it as if it had come into existence by means of "nature in the individual," or in other words by means of the artist's innate talent. In this sense, we will not be attending to the object as a product of design.

We may add to this that, in experiencing an artwork as the product of genius, we attend to it as if its production were not influenced by market forces. As Kant puts the point, there is a fundamental difference between the concepts of fine art and handicraft. The concept of handicraft is that of a "remunerative" practice that is appealing to the practitioner primarily because of the pay. This makes the practice one of labor, or "a business, which on its own account is disagreeable (drudgery)." By contrast, the concept of fine art is that of a "free" practice that is not tied to economic considerations. The artist's aim is not primarily to earn money, but to engage in a kind of "play," which is "an occupation which is agreeable on its own account."[38]

We know, of course, that in reality market forces have influenced the production of many of the artworks that we find beautiful, just as we know that in reality artists have followed rules of some sort or other in making the works that we find beautiful. As far as the latter point is concerned, we have seen that Kant acknowledges this quite explicitly when he writes that "every art presupposes rules which are laid down as the foundation which first enables a product, if it is to be called one of art, to be represented as possible."[39] To this he adds that "there is still no fine art in which something mechanical, capable of being at once comprehended and followed in obedience to rules, and consequently something *academic* does not constitute the essential condition of the art."[40] The essential point is that when we abstract and put aside our desire to understand the work's determinate internal end, we come to experience it for the time being as if these were not the realities. This goes hand in hand with opening ourselves up to experiencing the work's beauty.

Taking the account of genius to operate at an epistemological level amounts to taking it as an account according to which, once we carry out an appropriate act of abstraction, our ensuing experience of artistic beauty will be imbued with the representation of the work as a quasi-natural entity. Construed in this way, Kant's account of genius will turn out not to be unlike some of his other accounts of representations of finality. As we will see more fully in Chapter 6, for instance, he holds that it can be acceptable for us to seek out final causes in nature even though we do not know for certain that they exist. We are within our rights, Kant claims, in "applying the teleological estimate, at least problematically, to the investigation of nature" in our pursuit of explanations of natural phenomena.[41] In forming this kind of teleological estimate of nature, we treat what likely *lacks* a grounding in an agent's desire as if it *possesses* such a grounding. In the case of genius, exactly the reverse is true: we treat what likely possesses a grounding in an agent's desire as if it lacked such a grounding. Just as Kant holds that our taking a stance of design can perform the useful function of furthering our investigation of nature in the case of natural teleology, our adopting the stance of genius amounts to carrying out a useful function of abstraction that enables us to experience aesthetic pleasure in situations in which we might not otherwise have been able to do so.

Kant's view is that the most significant function of what he calls "fine art" is to enable its viewers to experience the pleasure of beauty. He categorizes "fine art" along with "agreeable art" as varieties of what he calls "aesthetic art." Aesthetic art, generally speaking, aims at pleasing us. In the case of agreeable art, the end of the art is "that the pleasure should accompany the representations considered as mere *sensations*." In the case of fine art, the end of the art is that the pleasure should accompany the representations "considered as *modes of cognition*."[42] Of course, from a contemporary perspective, we know that not all good art aims to please. For instance, although the artworks that make up Andy Warhol's *Death and Disaster* series may be artistically good, they were not intended to please. It is a mistake to think that art that aims at beauty, specifically, sits at the pinnacle of the enterprise of art.[43]

It is worth noting that the nature of the connection between the artist's intentions for a work and our experience of it may be somewhat complicated. Consider, for example, one of Marcel Duchamp's readymades, such as *Fountain*. This porcelain urinal was laid flat on its back, signed "R. Mutt," and sent in 1917 to an exhibition organized by the Society of Independent Artists (which promptly rejected it). Duchamp's own intention with this work was to move decisively away from what he called "retinal" art. With such art, he said in an interview, "you look at a painting for what you see, what comes on your retina; you add nothing intellectual to it."[44] His aim with the readymades, by contrast, was to choose an object "that would not attract me either by its beauty or by its ugliness, to find a point of indifference in my looking at it." Duchamp's aim, then, was diametrically opposed to the aim of producing fine art in Kant's sense. The complication, however, is that viewers have not always found themselves aesthetically indifferent to readymades such as *Fountain*. Some early critics experienced it as looking like a Madonna or a Buddha, and as revealing what is, in fact, a lovely form.[45] Even Duchamp, speaking of his own experience, has subsequently admitted that after 20 or 30 years of looking at a readymade such as *Fountain*, "you begin to like it."[46]

It is clearly possible to have an experience of beauty while engaging with an object even if its maker had not intended its primary function to be to enable such experiences – and even if the maker had deliberately set out to create a work that would *not* do so. What speaks against our approaching every artwork we encounter with the exclusive aim of experiencing it, if possible, as beautiful is that in doing so we miss out on other virtues it may possess. While it is valuable to have experiences of beauty, not least of all because of their contribution to our moral development, it does not follow that all art should aim to be beautiful.

Given that it is possible to experience the pleasure of beauty as part of our engagement with artworks, we can say that, ultimately, there is no reason to think that art's capacity for fostering our moral development is inferior to nature's. There perhaps remains a sense in which our experience of art is, as Murdoch puts it, more easily "degraded" than our experience of nature, if by this we mean that it can be more difficult to put aside our ordinary desires as we pursue artistic beauty. This is partly because of the kinds of contingent features of the artworld that Rousseau has pointed out, features which can lead us to overvalue our reputations and self-images as we pursue the arts. It is also partly because artworks tend to possess finality, and the fact that they appear to have been designed by makers introduces the risk that our desire to understand them will dominate our experience. As Kant emphasizes, however, this point does not only apply to artworks. We may be led to seek out teleological understandings of natural entities as well, and insofar as we do so, whatever pleasure we feel will not be disinterested. It is in order to deal with these potential obstacles to experiences of the pleasure of beauty that the notion of abstraction has a useful role to play in a Kantian aesthetic theory.

Notes

1 Iris Murdoch, *The Sovereignty of Good* (London: Ark Paperbacks, Routledge & Kegan Paul, 1985), 85.
2 CJ 5:354.
3 Rousseau, *Discourses*, 12.
4 Ibid., 8.
5 Ibid., 12.
6 CJ 5:298.
7 CJ 5:299–300.
8 CJ 5:210.
9 Anthropology 7:244. Similarly, in the *Observations*, Kant describes the "opinion that others may have of our value and their judgment of our actions" as "a motivation of great weight," and refers to honor as the "simulacrum of virtue" (Observations 2:218).
10 Morals 6:473–474.
11 Wood advances a similar interpretation, suggesting that Kant's view is that the pursuit of the arts can help us to become more sociable because it unites us in an enjoyable activity that is associated with a critical discourse in which we seek to bring our opinions into agreement with the opinions of others through a process of expression and communication; see Allen Wood, *Kant's Ethical Thought* (Cambridge: Cambridge University Press, 1999), 266.
12 CJ 5:297.
13 Idea 8:21.
14 Idea 8:21.
15 CJ 5:370.
16 Kant holds that it is a feature of the "form" of an object that invites us to experience it as artifactual rather than as natural. According to Kant, objects that we experience as artifactual manifest a "contingency of the form of the thing in relation to reason," whereas objects we experience as natural manifest a "necessity" of the form in relation to reason. Once we recognize a formal contingency, we are then drawn to "look upon the origin of the thing as if, just because of that contingency, it could only be possible through reason" (CJ 5:369–370).
17 See Chapter 3.
18 Kant understands "art in general" to be that which is produced "through freedom, i.e. through an act of will that places reason at the basis of its action" (which means that animal products, such as beehives, do not strictly speaking count as art) (CJ 5:303).
19 Paul Guyer takes up this issue in *Kant and the Claims of Taste* (Cambridge: Cambridge University Press, 1997), 198.

20   CJ 5:220.

21   CJ 5:220. Note that "*Zweckmäßigkeit*" is sometimes rendered as "purposiveness" in English translations of Kant.

22   At times, Kant uses "finality" to describe a property of a concept, rather than an object. For example, in the "Third Moment" of the *Critique of Judgment*, he claims that "the causality of a *concept* in respect of its *Object* is finality (*forma finalis*)" (CJ 5:220).

23   CJ 5:231.

24   CJ 5:270. Kant discusses these examples of abstraction in the context of his discussion of the pleasure of sublimity, but they serve equally well to illustrate the notion of abstraction in cases of beauty.

25   CJ 5:229.

26   CJ 5:307–308.

27   CJ 5:308.

28   CJ 5:308.

29   CJ 5:309.

30   Strictly speaking, of course, there is a sense in which nobody, whether acting through genius or not, knows how ideas have entered his or her head. Along these lines, it does not seem that there is reason to limit genius to art, as Kant seeks to do; see Peter Kivy, *The Possessor and the Possessed: Handel, Mozart, Beethoven, and the Idea of Musical Genius* (New Haven: Yale University Press, 2001), 111.

31   CJ 5:307.

32   See, for example, Eva Schaper, "Taste, Sublimity, and Genius," in *The Cambridge Companion to Kant*, ed. Paul Guyer (Cambridge: Cambridge University Press, 1992), 389; Peter Lewis, "'Original Nonsense': Art and Genius in Kant's Aesthetic," in *Kant and His Influence*, ed. G. MacDonald Ross and T. McWalter (Bristol: Thoemmes, 1990), 127–128; and Paul Guyer, "Interest, Nature, and Art: A Problem in Kant's Aesthetics," *Review of Metaphysics*, 31 (1978): 598.

33   Henry Allison points out that Kant seems to have committed a *non sequitur* in supposing that the fact that judgments of artistic beauty must be free from certain forms of conceptualization entails that artworks themselves must have any particular source; see *Kant's Theory of Taste: A Reading of the Critique of Aesthetic Judgment* (Cambridge: Cambridge University Press, 2001), 280.

34   See my article "Kant on Genius and Art," *British Journal of Aesthetics* 47, no. 2 (2007): 207. There is, of course, a question concerning what sorts of understanding might be relevant to experiencing the pleasure of beauty while engaging with an object, and, specifically, a question concerning the extent to which an understanding of the work as a copy might be

relevant to such an experience. While it may matter to my experience of an object's beauty – because it matters to the character of my experience of its subjective finality – that I know that it is a painting rather than, say, a photograph, it seems to matter less that I know that it is an original painting as opposed to a copy. The reason, perhaps, lies in the fact that the relevant category, as far as my experience of its beauty is concerned, is something like the category of "painting." And, of course, both the original and the copy belong to this category.

35 CJ 5:307.
36 CJ 5:306.
37 CJ 5:307.
38 CJ 5:304.
39 CJ 5:307.
40 CJ 5:310.
41 CJ 5:360.
42 CJ 5:305. Interestingly, if the proper function of fine art is to enable spectators to have experiences of the pleasure of beauty, then a spectator might experience the pleasure of *goodness* upon recognizing that a particular artwork enables him or her to enjoy the pleasure beauty.
43 As Dominic McIver Lopes points out, the distinction between "aesthetic value" and "artistic value" is not necessarily as straightforward as it might seem, especially in light of the development of Avant-Garde art. See *Beyond Art* (Oxford: Oxford University Press, 2014), ch. 5.
44 Marcel Duchamp, interview by Joan Bakewell, *The Late Show*, BBC, June 15, 1968.
45 See Jerrold E. Seigel, *The Private Worlds of Marcel Duchamp* (Berkeley: University of California Press, 1995), 137.
46 Marcel Duchamp, *The Late Show*.

5

Sublimity and Esteem

Not to Disavow the Moral Self-Esteem of Such a Being

Just as Kant's account of the pleasure of beauty is intertwined with his broader ethical priorities, so too is his account of the pleasure of sublimity. And just as Kant holds that beauty's connection with our emotional life, and specifically with the emotion of love, makes its pursuit conducive to our moral development by helping us to distance ourselves from our inclinations, so too does he hold that sublimity's connection with our emotional life makes it conducive to this end. The difference, on Kant's account, is that instead of being connected with love, sublimity is connected with respect or esteem. Thus, in the passage from Section 29 of the third *Critique* which we have already partially considered, Kant claims not only that the pleasure of beauty "prepares us to love something, even nature, apart from any interest," but also that the pleasure of sublimity prepares us "to esteem something highly even in opposition to our (sensuous) interest."[1] A first question, then, is why developing our capacity for esteem might serve our moral development. A second question is whether we have good reason to

The Possibility of Culture: Pleasure and Moral Development in Kant's Aesthetics, First Edition. Bradley Murray.
© 2015 John Wiley & Sons, Inc. Published 2015 by John Wiley & Sons, Inc.

accept Kant's view that the experience of sublimity is, in fact, closely connected with esteem.

It is possible, in the first place, to distinguish three different roles that Kant takes feelings of respect and esteem to be capable of playing in moral life. The first emerges most clearly in the *Critique of Practical Reason*. We considered, in Chapter 2, Kant's distinction between practical and pathological versions of the feeling of love. The same distinction will apply to the feeling of respect. In the second *Critique*'s account of moral motivation, Kant has practical respect, specifically, in mind.[2] As human animals, he claims, we can "never be altogether free from desires and inclinations which, because they rest on physical causes, do not of themselves accord with the moral law."[3] Overcoming these desires and inclinations inevitably involves "inner necessitation to what one does not altogether like to do," and one way to bring this about is through feeling practical respect for the moral law itself.[4] In complying with the moral law out of respect, we can expect to feel an accompanying feeling of "dread," even if, at the same time, we hold the law in high esteem.[5]

The second role that Kant takes a feeling of respect to be capable of playing in moral life emerges in the *Observations*. Here, Kant conceives respect to be a pathological rather than practical feeling. Specifically, he takes it to be a feeling of the dignity of human nature. Such a feeling, he claims, "lives in every human breast."[6] Like pathological love, Kant takes pathological respect to help us to resist our personal inclinations and to act with greater impartiality. In love, we are able to resist our inclinations because we feel affectionately toward others and wish to see them benefit. In respect, we are able to resist our inclinations because we have the feeling that they possess dignity and do not want them to end up in situations that compromise this dignity.

The first two roles that feelings of respect can play in moral life are, ultimately, less directly relevant to Kant's account of the pleasure of sublimity than the third. In this role, a feeling of respect or esteem is directed toward certain aspects of *oneself* – which makes it a feeling of self-respect or self-esteem (*Selbstschätzung*).[7] To better understand this notion of self-esteem, it will help to attend to the section of the *Metaphysics of Morals* entitled "On Servility." There, Kant begins by considering the value of personhood: a person, he claims, is "not to be valued merely as a means to the ends of others or even to his own ends, but as an end in itself," which is to say that a person "possesses a *dignity* (an absolute inner worth) by which he exacts *respect* for himself from all other rational beings in the world."[8] Beyond being entitled to respect from other rational beings, Kant claims, persons are to value and respect *themselves* insofar as they are persons. When someone recognizes his rational nature, Kant claims, "there comes *exaltation* of the highest self-esteem, the feeling of his inner worth (*valor*), in terms of which he is above any price (*pretium*) and possesses an inalienable dignity (*dignitas interna*), which instills in him respect for himself (*reverentia*)."[9] Kant's underlying thought is that, to the extent that we are capable of feeling such self-esteem as rational beings, we will be better able to resist our inclinations. Specifically, "worldly" concerns, including the concern to satisfy our inclinations, will come to seem relatively trivial to us when we consider them alongside our rational natures.[10]

In claiming that our personhood, and resulting dignity, derive from the rational aspects of ourselves, Kant also specifies that these do not derive from our sensible natures, or from aspects of ourselves that are connected with our status as human animals. In fact, Kant claims that it is appropriate to value ourselves by a low standard when we are thinking of ourselves as such animals:

> Humanity in his person is the object of the respect which he can demand from every other human being, but which he must also not forfeit. Hence he can and should value himself by a low as well as by a high standard, depending on whether he views himself as a sensible being (in terms of his animal nature) or as an intelligible being (in terms of his moral predisposition). Since he must regard himself not only as a person generally but also as a *human being*, that is, as a person who has duties his own reason lays upon him, his insignificance as a *human animal* may not infringe upon his consciousness of his dignity as a *rational human being*, and he should not disavow the moral self-esteem of such a being ...[11]

In Kant's view, then, our self-esteem should be divided. On the one hand, we should have a high moral self-esteem – that is, a high-self esteem insofar as we consider ourselves as rational beings capable of acting on moral principles. On the other hand, we should have a low self-esteem insofar as we are human animals.

As mentioned earlier, Kant's tendency to disparage the "animal" aspects of human beings is controversial. In light of this fact, the best way to proceed in reconstructing Kant's account of sublimity will be to avoid taking on unneeded presuppositions about the distinction between animality and rationality. In fact, many of these presuppositions are not central to a Kantian framework for understanding the experience of sublimity. What is central, however, is his claim that in its structure, our motivation is divided. On the one hand, we have inclinations that lead us to act in ways that often leave out the needs of others. On the other hand, we have the capacity to reflect on ourselves and on our inclinations in order ultimately to resist them, and we may, moreover, feel esteem toward this reflective aspect of ourselves.

Before turning to Kant's account of sublimity itself, it is worth noting one further area of potential controversy that surrounds it. Kant seeks at times to incorporate controversial elements of his transcendental idealism into his account of what it means for us to have rational natures, and this feeds directly into his account of sublimity. For instance, sometimes he talks as if recognizing our true natures as rational human beings involves becoming aware of "supersensible" aspects of ourselves, which Kant takes to be aspects of ourselves that are not subject to natural laws.[12] Thus, Kant claims that one source of the self-esteem that we discover during certain experiences of sublimity comes from the recognition that we possess "a faculty that is itself supersensible,"[13] and he describes the feeling that we have in an experience of sublimity as making us "alive to the feeling of the supersensible side of our being."[14] Just as there are advantages to reconstructing Kant's account of sublimity in a way that does not invoke the extraneous claim that we are to devalue the animal side of our nature, there are advantages to reconstructing the account in a way that does not invoke extraneous metaphysical claims about the self. This is possible since what is essential to Kant's account does not depend on these metaphysical claims. Of course, even if reconstructing Kant's account of sublimity without them yields a view that is less controversial than it might otherwise be, this does not mean that the account succeeds in the end. Indeed, we will see that what is most controversial about it goes deeper than this.

A Might of the Mind

Kant holds that, whereas an object that we find beautiful seems to us to convey "a finality in its form making the object appear, as it were, pre-adapted to our power of judgement, so that it thus forms of itself an object of our delight," an object that we find sublime seems instead to convey a "contra-finality" in its form. The latter sort of object appears, Kant suggests, to "contravene the ends of our power of judgement, to be ill-adapted to our faculty of presentation, and to be, as it were, an outrage on the imagination, and yet it is judged all the more sublime on that account."[15]

Although this notion of contra-finality is central to Kant's account of sublimity, invoking it alone does not fully explain why the state is pleasurable. The next aspect of Kant's account is that our experience of contra-finality prompts us to recognize an aspect of ourselves that somehow exceeds in stature the experienced hindrance. As Kant puts it, what we call sublime "in external nature, or even internal nature (e.g. certain affects) is only represented as a might of the mind enabling it to overcome this or that hindrance of sensibility."[16] This part of our-selves is precisely our rational nature – it is the aspect of ourselves that is capable of the kind of self-reflection needed to act on principles and to oppose inclinations.

Why, though, should experiencing contra-finality prompt us to rec-ognize our rational natures? In order to answer this question, we must note, first of all, that it is an enduring theme in Kant's thought that there is insight to be gained from experiences in which we feel humbled or humiliated by mighty forces. In the *Critique of Practical Reason*, for instance, Kant considers the experience of being humiliated by the moral law as exemplified in a "humble common man in whom I perceive uprightness of character in a higher degree than I am aware of in myself."[17] Before a person like this, Kant claims, "*my spirit bows.*"[18] Observing such a person challenges our self-conceit and helps us to rec-ognize the aspects of ourselves that ground our own dignity. These, specifically, are those aspects of ourselves that are connected with our capacity for moral action.[19]

Just as Kant holds that we can experience humiliation upon being reminded of the moral law, he also holds that we can experience this feeling when we experience contra-finality as we engage with various phenomena. The pleasure that we feel in an experience of sublimity accompanies our feeling of heightened self-esteem, which arises as we recognize the strength that inheres in our rational nature. Thus, Kant's account entails that we actually take pleasure in an aspect of *ourselves* while we are experiencing sublimity. This is why Kant describes sublimity as characterized by a "subreption," or a "substitution of a respect for the Object in place of one for the idea of humanity in our own self."[20] If the pleasure of sublimity really does involve such a subreption, then it will be correct to say, as Kant does, that sublimity "does not reside in any of the things of nature, but only in our own mind, insofar as we may become conscious of our superiority over nature within, and thus also over nature without us (as exerting influence upon us)."[21]

Kant, himself, poses a question that his account of sublimity naturally raises, namely the question of how something that is "apprehended as inherently contra-final" can at the same time be "noted with an expression of approval."[22] Kant's answer, we are seeing, is that it is precisely because there is an initial, displeasurable, experience of contra-finality in an experience of sublimity that a pleasurable experience can ensue. And yet, the experience of sublimity has a mixed character on Kant's account. This means that Kant is not in a position to describe it as a purely pleasurable experience, as he describes the experience of beauty. Thus, he writes that whereas the pleasure of beauty is one that is "directly attended with a feeling of the furtherance of life," the pleasure of sublimity is a "negative pleasure." In the case of sublimity, there is an initial "check to the vital forces," and "the mind is not simply attracted by the object, but is also alternately repelled thereby," making the pleasure of sublimity "not sport, but dead earnest in the affairs of the imagination."[23]

Kant divides experiences of sublimity into those of "external nature" and those of "internal nature." Experiences of sublimity belonging to the category of external nature include those of mathematical and dynamical sublimity. In the case of mathematical sublimity, to begin with, the experienced contra-finality results from the representation of a vast magnitude. Roughly speaking, in representing such a magnitude, we feel that, try as we might, we will never be able fully to perceive it. The magnitude seems to us to be too vast for our perceptual capacities as human beings. As Kant puts it, "[i]n the immeasurableness of nature and the inadequacy of our faculty for adopting a standard proportionate to the aesthetic estimation of the magnitude of its realm, we [find] our own limitation."[24]

Kant's explanation of the experience of mathematical sublimity depends partly on his claim that we must engage in a process of synthesis in order to form representations of entities whose parts we cannot experience all at once. The synthetic process that Kant describes here will be different from the process that he describes in the first *Critique*'s first edition transcendental deduction, which we considered briefly in Chapter 3. The primary difference is that, whereas Kant earlier invoked the process of synthesis in order to explain how it is possible for us to represent objectivity, as such – that is, how it is possible for a stream of purely subjective representations that are not initially united in the representation of an object to gain such unity – he is now invoking a version of this process in order to explain how we might represent what we experience as parts of objects as belonging to larger objects. Thus, the units that we apprehend are now taken already to be imbued with objectivity in the relevant sense.

The relevant synthetic process is one that involves acts of "apprehension" and "comprehension." In order for us to represent a large object, such as an Egyptian pyramid, Kant claims, we must carry out a process involving both kinds of act. The initially apprehended parts will be tiers of stones. But in order for us to get a sense of the magnitude of the pyramid as a whole, we must carry out acts of comprehension in which, as it were, we hold together in our minds the various parts that we have apprehended.[25] Kant's point is that there are limits to our capacities for apprehension and comprehension, and our efforts to represent large magnitudes bring these limits to light. When it comes to apprehension, it is obvious that we face limits resulting from the nature of our perceptual systems. We are, for example, unable to see all of a large pyramid at once. When it comes to comprehension, Kant takes our limits, broadly speaking, to have to do with our memories. As he puts it, "if the apprehension has reached a point beyond which the representations of sensuous intuition in the case of the parts first apprehended begin to disappear from the imagination as this advances to the apprehension of yet others, as much, then is lost at one end as is gained at the other, and for comprehension we get a maximum which the imagination cannot exceed." In the case of the pyramid, specifically, we need time to apprehend it stone by stone, but, Kant claims, "in this interval the first tiers always in part disappear before the imagination has taken in the last, and so the comprehension is never complete." Generally speaking, Kant holds, there is a "maximum which the imagination cannot exceed," or in other words, there is "an absolute measure beyond which no greater is possible subjectively (i.e. for the judging Subject)."[26]

If engaging with an object such as a pyramid can, at least under certain circumstances, make clear the limitations of our imaginations, then we can expect that engaging with even larger objects will bring the point home more forcefully. Kant seeks to explain this idea by invoking the notion of measurement. If we continue to consider ever-larger magnitudes, Kant claims, we move from magnitudes that we are more capable of grasping to those that seem simply impossible for us to grasp, so that standards of measurement will eventually become meaningless to us. For instance, we can grasp the height of a tree because it is not much greater than the height of a human being; we can grasp the height of a mountain because it is the height of such-and-such many trees; we can grasp the earth's diameter because it is as long as the height of such-and-such many mountains; and so on. But as we continue this list, it becomes ever more difficult truly to grasp the magnitude of the relevant objects, since "in our onward advance we always arrive at proportionately greater units."[27] When, finally, we attempt to contemplate the size of the cosmos as a whole, Kant suggests, it will seem to us to be *absolutely great* no matter what vantage point we occupy and no matter what unit of measurement we adopt. Its magnitude will be one that we are simply unable to grasp. We feel as if we are facing the onset of a never-ending process that we are incapable of completing, which involves a "feeling of the effort towards a comprehension that exceeds the faculty of imagination for mentally grasping the progressive apprehension in a whole of intuition."[28] Our attempts at grasping large magnitudes, then, provoke "break downs" of the faculty of imagination. In so doing they reveal our own cognitive inadequacy and humiliate us insofar as we had previously harbored the feeling that the universe is somehow within our grasp.[29]

According to Kant, the element of contra-finality that is part of an experience of mathematical sublimity prompts us to recognize that there is actually a way in which we are capable of conceiving of the relevant synthetic processes of apprehension and comprehension as complete. This is not by employing our perceptual capacities, but by employing our capacity for rationality. Reason, Kant claims, "requires totality, and consequently comprehension in *one* intuition," and demands that we regard the infinite magnitude "as *completely given*."[30] Kant's point is that we are capable of forming the idea of an infinite magnitude in spite of the fact that we have never succeeded in perceiving such a magnitude. Insofar as it enables us to recognize that our rational capacities operate to some extent independently of the sensible world – the world in which vast objects are located – and independently of our sensible inclinations, the experience of mathematical sublimity challenges our self-conceit as sensible beings, and provides an opportunity to feel heightened self-esteem as we recognize the preeminence of our rational capacities. This feeling of self-esteem accounts for both the pleasurable aspect of the experience, as well as its capacity to foster our long-term moral development.

In the case of dynamical sublimity, we experience contra-finality as a consequence of representing the phenomenon with which we are engaging as possessing a great deal of might. As Kant puts it:

> [b]old, overhanging, and, as it were, threatening rocks, thunderclouds piled up the vault of heaven, borne along with flashes and peals, volcanoes in all their violence of destruction, hurricanes leaving desolation in their track, the boundless ocean rising with rebellious force, the high waterfall of some mighty river, and the like, make our power of resistance of trifling moment in comparison with their might.[31]

Kant specifies that he is not suggesting that we are actually afraid of such mighty phenomena while we are experiencing them as dynamically sublime. He distinguishes between looking upon an object as fearful, on the one hand, and fearing the object, on the other hand. Experiencing something as fearful without being afraid of it is a matter of "simply *picturing to ourselves* the case of our wishing to offer some resistance to it, and recognizing that all such resistance would be quite futile." In fact, Kant claims, it is necessary that we not actually fear the object, because doing so will likely interfere with our having a pleasurable aesthetic experience to begin with. Rather than continuing to contemplate an object of which we are afraid, we are instead inclined to flee; it is impossible, Kant claims, to "delight in terror that is seriously entertained."[32]

Encountering the mighty object humiliates exaggerated beliefs that we might have concerning our own power as embodied beings, forcing upon us "the recognition of our physical helplessness as beings of nature."[33] But the experience also brings to light the fact that there are aspects of ourselves – again, our rational capacities – which can operate without regard for our physical well-being. In this way, the experience of dynamical sublimity provides us with an opportunity "to regard as small those things of which we are wont to be solicitous (worldly goods, health, and life)," and to focus instead on "our highest principles."[34] It is this change of focus, or subreption, that ultimately, Kant suggests, "saves humanity in our own person from humiliation."[35]

Experiences of sublimity in internal nature, like experiences of sublimity in external nature, arise alongside experiences of contra-finality; Kant claims, as we have seen, that what we call sublime "in external nature, or even internal nature (e.g. certain affects) is only represented as a might of the mind enabling it to overcome this or that hindrance of sensibility." Experiences of sublimity in internal nature have to do, specifically, with our experience of mental states arising in ourselves or in others.[36] For example, according to Kant, anger and desperation – the latter in the form of "the rage of forlorn hope," but not mere "faint-hearted despair" – excite "the consciousness of our power of overcoming every resistance." These states are "affects," on Kant's scheme for categorizing mental states, and more specifically, affects "of the strenuous type."[37] A "strenuous" affect is precisely one that can make us conscious of our capacity to overcome hindrances or resistances. When we experience a strenuous affect such as anger in ourselves, or observe it in someone else, we may form a representation of the overcoming of a hindrance – perhaps, say, an injustice – which, in turn, may lead us to recognize our capacity actually to overcome such a hindrance. The recognition of the fact that we have this capacity will, on Kant's account, go hand in hand with a pleasurable feeling of self-esteem. What Kant calls "languid" affects, by contrast, do not make us conscious of our capacity to overcome hindrances. For instance, when we are experiencing a mere "sympathetic grief that refuses to be consoled," or a grief that has to do with an imaginary misfortune that we have suffered, we are in no way inspired to recognize our power of overcoming hindrances.

Another mental state that Kant takes to be sublime is the feeling of disappointment with humanity. Kant is careful to point out that this feeling is not the same as full-blown misanthropy, which is a feeling of outright enmity toward our fellow human beings. Nor is it the same as "anthrophobia," which is the shunning of others because we imagine that they are against us. Disappointment with humanity is more benign than these other states, and is common in "right-minded" people as they age; it is the result of "long and sad experience," and is rooted in dashed hopes for humanity:

> Falsehood, ingratitude, injustice, the puerility of the ends which we our-
> selves look upon as great and momentous, and to attain which we inflict
> upon our fellow human beings all imaginable evils – these all so contradict
> the idea of what people might be if they only would, and are so at variance
> with our active wish to see them better, that, to avoid hating where we
> cannot love, it seems but a slight sacrifice to forgo all the joys of fellowship
> with our kind.[38]

Thus, disappointment with humanity is at bottom a feeling of sad-ness over the ills that human beings inflict on each other. It is connected with sublimity, Kant claims, insofar it is "founded on ideas," and, specifically, on moral ones.[39] As an affective state that is founded on moral ideas – including a moral concern for impartiality and equality – it is, in Kant's view, inherently connected with our rational capacities. Kant's view is that when we encounter this state in ourselves or another, we may, through a subreption, come to recog-nize our rational natures, and feel a pleasurable, empowering esteem for ourselves that can contribute to our capacity to act in opposition to our sensible inclinations.

Like the mental state of disappointment with humanity, Kant takes the mental state of enthusiasm to be founded on moral ideas. He defines "enthusiasm" as "the idea of the good connected with affect," and elu-cidates this notion partly by contrasting it with fanaticism.[40] Unlike enthusiasm, Kant claims, fanaticism is characterized by delusion, namely "a *delusion* that would *will some* VISION *beyond all the bounds of sensi-bility*, i.e. would dream according to principles (rational raving)." Whereas enthusiasm is comparable to "delirium," fanaticism has a looser tie to reality, and is instead comparable to "mania." Whereas enthusiasm is "a transitory state to which the healthiest understanding is liable to become at times the victim," fanaticism is an "undermining disease."[41] Kant has mixed feelings concerning whether it is healthy for us to feel enthusiasm. We see this ambivalence not only in the third *Critique*, but also, for instance, in his *Essay on the Maladies of the Head*, which addresses the classification of mental disorders. There, he describes enthusiasm as the "appearance of fantasy in moral sensations that are in themselves good."[42] Individuals who are "more excited by a moral sensation than by a principle, and this to a larger extent than others could imagine according to their own insipid and often ignoble feeling," will be widely considered by these others to be fantasts.[43] The "fantast," he now adds, manifests a type of mental "derangement" in which his or her imagination has taken over.

In spite of his tendency to speak of enthusiasm as if it were a kind of mental disorder, Kant also holds that it can be in some ways beneficial to us. He writes, for example, that "nothing great has ever been accomplished in the world without [enthusiasm]."[44] In the *Conflict of the Faculties*, Kant claims that witnessing the French revolution is apt to raise in "the hearts of all spectators (who are not engaged in this game themselves) a wishful participation that borders closely on enthusiasm the very expression of which is fraught with danger." What these onlookers are feeling is ultimately grounded in moral ideas, since genuine enthusiasm, he claims, "always moves only toward what is ideal and, indeed, to what is purely moral, such as the concept of right."[45] The fact that Kant sees enthusiasm not simply as a "malady of the head," but also as connected with difficult and dangerous revolutionary acts of resistance grounded in moral concern begins to explain why he takes it to be a sublime mental state. "From an aesthetic point of view," he writes in the third *Critique*, "enthusiasm is sublime, because it is an effort of one's powers called forth by ideas which give to the mind an impetus of far stronger and more enduring efficacy than the stimulus afforded by sensible representations."[46] When we feel enthusiasm or witness it in another, we may be led, through a subreption, to recognize our rational capacities, and thereby to recognize an aspect of ourselves that is not bound up with our inclinations.[47]

A final example of a sublime mental state is that of freedom from affect "in a mind that strenuously follows its unswerving principles."[48] Kant praises apathy in the *Anthropology*, writing that the gift of apathy is a "fortunate phlegm (in the moral sense)." Those who lack the relevant kind of apathy tend to go wrong because they do not reflect sufficiently on their feeling states. Specifically, they do not compare the current feeling "with the sum of all feelings (of pleasure or displeasure)."[49] Similarly, in the *Metaphysics of Morals*, Kant describes moral apathy as a mental state that arises when a person is able to govern internal states through reflection. In this way, the person manages "to bring all his capacities and inclinations under his (reason's) control and so to rule over himself."[50] Although apathy, unlike the other sublime mental states that we have considered, is characterized by its lack of affect, sublime mental states all have in common that they are helpful in confronting sensible hindrances. Kant's underlying thought is that, when we observe ourselves or someone else in a state that is free from affect while also acting in accordance with moral principles, we may be led, as in the other cases, to carry out the subreption that he takes to underlie both the pleasure of sublimity and its potential to foster our moral development.

It may initially seem as if there is little sense to be made of the notion of an experience of artistic sublimity, especially if we are guided solely by a remark that Kant makes in the course of his discussion of mathematical sublimity in the Analytic of the Sublime. There, he advises us not to expect that our engagement with artifacts will yield "pure" experiences of mathematical sublimity, since these are such that "a human end determines the form as well as the magnitude."[51] A pure experience of mathematical sublimity must, by contrast, have "no end belonging to the object as its determining ground."

In spite of Kant's own reservations, his account does, ultimately, seem capable of accommodating experiences of artistic sublimity. First, Kant speaks here only of the impossibility of "pure" experiences of artistic mathematical sublimity. However, there could still be "impure" experiences of mathematical sublimity in response to artworks. In such cases, our pleasure would be grounded partly on our understanding of the object's internal end.[52] In fact, Kant even discusses two kinds of experiences that appear to constitute examples of impure sublimity: the experiences of the "monstrous" and of the "colossal." In the case of the monstrous, the object "by its size ... defeats the end that forms its concept."[53] The object, in other words, seems to be too much for what it is supposed to be.[54] In the case of the colossal, we likewise experience the object as oversized – but not to the extent that we do in the case of the monstrous. The colossal is "almost too great for presentation" and thus only "relatively monstrous."[55] In both cases, however, our representing the object's end is a necessary part of our resulting experience. If it is possible for us to experience impure sublimity insofar as our pleasure is grounded in a teleological representation of the object, this will closely mirror Kant's claim that it is possible for us to experience dependent beauty insofar as our pleasure is grounded in such a representation.

It is open to Kant to suggest, moreover, that to the extent that an object manifests finality, and so appears to have been made, we may carry out an act of abstraction in order to put ourselves in a position to enjoy experiences approaching those of "pure" sublimity. In fact, Kant suggests that it will sometimes even be necessary to abstract when we seek to experience the sublimity of natural phenomena. In a passage that we alluded to in Chapter 4, Kant writes:

> So, if we call the sight of the starry heaven *sublime*, we must not found our judgement of it upon any concepts of worlds inhabited by rational beings, with the bright spots, which we see filling the space above us, as their suns moving in orbits prescribed for them with the wisest regard to ends. ... Similarly, as to the prospect of the ocean, we are not to regard it as we, with our minds stored with knowledge on a variety of matters (which, however, is not contained in the immediate intuition), are accustomed to represent it in *thought*, as, let us say, a spacious realm of aquatic creatures, or as the mighty reservoirs from which are drawn the vapours that fill the air with clouds of moisture for the good of the land, or yet as an element which no doubt divides continent from continent, but at the same time affords the means of the greatest commercial intercourse between them – for in this way we get nothing beyond teleological judgements.[56]

To be thinking, for instance, of the movements of the stars as if they had been preconceived by a cosmic maker, or of the ocean's contribution to the ecosystem as if it had been preconceived by such an agent would be to engage in a type of intellectual activity that is not compatible with the experience of pure sublimity. To avoid these thoughts, we may abstract – in which case we would be experiencing these phenomena "as the poets do, according to what the impression upon the eye reveals."[57]

Kant himself invokes two artifactual examples in describing the experience of mathematical sublimity: the example of Savary's observations of Egyptian pyramids, and the example of St. Peter's in Rome. When one observes such buildings, one finds that one's cognitive capacities are overwhelmed, and, on the surface, at any rate, Kant seems to be suggesting that these amount to experiences of sublimity – which perhaps suggests that the observer has successfully abstracted from thoughts of the objects as having determinate internal ends.

Kant's primary doubts concerning artistic sublimity occur in the context of his discussion of mathematical sublimity. Even if these doubts are, in the end, to be taken seriously, they do not directly speak against the possibility that we might have experiences of dynamical sublimity or sublimity in internal nature as we engage with artworks. To take just the case of dynamical sublimity, there is every reason to think that it is possible for us to experience an artifact as mighty. Human artifacts can be just as destructive to us as natural objects. There is no reason, for example, why an artist could not make a dangerous artwork which spectators experienced as threatening to overpower them. The experience of encountering such an object would be no less overwhelming simply because we knew it to have been designed by a human being. Even literary descriptions of mighty phenomena can seem capable of provoking experiences of sublimity. Along these lines, Kant suggests in the *Observations* that "the description of a raging storm, or the depiction of the kingdom of hell by Milton arouses satisfaction, but with dread."[58]

Thus, we have at first glance every reason to think that Kant's theory of sublimity can be developed further than he does so in order to accommodate not just experiences of natural sublimity, but also those of artistic sublimity.[59]

By a Certain Subreption

If successful, Kant's account of sublimity will offer a wide-ranging explanation of experiences of sublimity that we may have in response to external nature, internal nature, and artifacts. Most importantly, it will explain why the pleasure of sublimity, in virtue of its connection with the feeling of self-esteem, can contribute to our moral development – that is, it will explain how sublimity prepares us "to esteem something highly even in opposition to our (sensuous) interest," and how its doing so makes it "final in reference to the moral feeling."[60]

The trouble, however, is that all of these explanations rest on one crucial, yet phenomenologically dubious claim, namely the claim that a subreption lies at the core of any given experience of sublimity. This is dubious insofar as it certainly does not feel as though we are taking pleasure in an aspect of ourselves – rational or otherwise – while we are experiencing sublimity. Instead, our experience is of being pleased by the object itself.

It is, to be sure, a mixed pleasure, since there may be feelings such as fear, insignificance, and desperation mixed in. Kant is right in this aspect of his characterization of the experience. However, it is entirely possible to hold that the experience of sublimity is a mixed one in this way without also holding that the experience is characterized by a split between an outer object, which is displeasing, and an inner object, which is pleasing. Given that Kant's explanation of the source of the pleasure in an experience of sublimity does not accord with the way things seem to us as we are actually having this experience, we would expect that he would offer us a compelling reason for adopting the explanation. However, he does little beyond asserting it, and when presented with such an assertion, we are bound to be left unconvinced.[61] Thus, Kant cannot, in the end, be said to have established that there is a close connection between the experience of sublimity and a feeling of esteem for our rational capacities, or to have established that the pursuit of experiences of sublimity is a way of developing morally by enabling us to strengthen our rational self-esteem.

This is not to say, however, that the experience of sublimity has no moral significance. Like the experience of beauty, the experience of sublimity is a pleasurable, disinterested experience characterized by detachment from the pleasing object. As Kant puts it, beauty and sublimity "agree on the point of pleasing on their own account."[62] In this way, these pleasures differ from the pleasures of goodness and agreeableness. Experiences of the pleasure of goodness are characterized by a desire to understand the object to an extent that experiences of beauty and sublimity are not. And whereas the pleasure of agreeableness draws us further into our senses leading us to become more attached to the sensible object and more consumed by inclinations that we have in relation to it, the pleasures of beauty and sublimity enable us to leave our sensory desires aside. Thus, because the experience of sublimity, like the experience of beauty, is an experience that is both disinterested and pleasurable, pursuing it can serve our moral development, providing us with a way of learning to distance ourselves from our inclinations without "too violent a leap."

Notes

1 CJ 5:267.
2 Kant emphasizes that practical respect is "produced solely by reason" (CPrR 5:76). The present interpretation is, broadly speaking, compatible with

Henry Allison's, which emphasizes the role of the non-feeling component of respect in the motivation of actions carried out from duty. What matters most when it comes to such motivation, Allison claims, is the recognition of the law's "supremely authoritative character, which is to be taken to mean that it provides a reason for action that outweighs or overrides all other reasons, particularly those stemming from one's desires" (*Kant's Theory of Freedom* [Cambridge: Cambridge University Press, 1990], 123). For a general overview of these issues, see Iain Morrisson, *Kant and the Role of Pleasure in Moral Action* (Athens: Ohio University Press, 2008).

3   CPrR 5:84.
4   CPrR 5:83–84.
5   CPrR 5:84.
6   Observations 2:217.
7   Morals 6:399.
8   Morals 6:435. Cf. Groundwork 4:428; Groundwork 4:438.
9   Morals 6:435–437.
10   CJ 5:261–262.
11   Morals: 6:435.
12   For example, in the *Critique of Pure Reason*, Kant takes up the issue of "transcendental" freedom: "It is especially noteworthy that it is this transcendental idea of freedom on which the practical concept of freedom is grounded, and the former constitutes the real moment of the difficulties in the latter, which have long surrounded the question if its possibility. Freedom in the practical sense is the independence of the power of choice from necessitation by impulses of sensibility. For a power of choice is sensible insofar as it is pathologically affected (through moving-causes of sensibility); it is called an animal power of choice (*arbitrium brutum*) if it can be pathologically necessitated. The human power of choice is indeed an *arbitrium sensitivum* [sensible power of choice], yet not *brutum* but *liberum*, because sensibility does not render its action necessary, but in the human being there is a faculty of determining oneself from oneself, independently of necessitation by sensible impulses" (A533/B561–A534/B562).

For more on Kant's notion of transcendental freedom see, e.g., Karl Ameriks, "Kant's Deduction of Freedom and Morality," *Journal of the History of Philosophy* 19, no. 1 (2008): 53–79, and Allison, *Kant's Theory of Freedom*.
13   CJ 5:254. Cf. CJ 5:255.
14   CJ 5:257–258.
15   CJ 5:245.
16   CJ 5:277.
17   CPrR 5:76–77.

18 CPrR 5:77.

19 Kant returns to this theme in the *Metaphysics of Morals*, where he describes moral humility as consisting in "[t]he consciousness and feeling of the insignificance of one's moral worth *in comparison with the* law." He contrasts moral humility with moral arrogance, which he describes as "a conviction of the greatness of one's moral worth, but only from failure to compare it with the law" (Morals 6:435–437).

20 CJ 5:257. In fact, Kant's view is that it is only possible to feel respect toward human beings; as he puts it in the second *Critique*, "[r]espect is always directed only to persons, never to things" (CPrR 5:76). Robert Clewis suggests that subreption is not essential to experiences of sublimity, by which he means that subjects can come consciously to recognize that the source of the pleasure that is being attributed to the object does not lie in the object itself, but within their own mind (*The Kantian Sublime and the Revelation of Freedom* [Cambridge: Cambridge University Press, 2009], 61). It is an interesting question just which aspects of this recognition may occur consciously, and which may occur unconsciously, on Kant's view. There is certainly at least some plausibility to Clewis's model, which appears to incorporate unconscious processes which may become conscious.

21 CJ 5:264. Kant's account of sublimity is grounded in the idea that the pleasurable aspect of the experience derives from our becoming aware of an aspect of ourselves that we experience to manifest "superiority" over sensible hindrances. But, Kant holds, it is important to distinguish between a person's "feeling for his sublime vocation, that is, his *elation of spirit* (*elatio animi*) or esteem for himself," on the one hand, and a person's "*self-conceit* (*arrogantia*), which is the "very opposite of true *humility* (*humilitas moralis*)" (Morals 6:437). On Kant's view, self-esteem is a precondition for being a moral agent in the first place. That is, according to Kant, there are certain moral endowments "such that anyone lacking them could have no duty to acquire them," and these include "*moral feeling, conscience, love* of one's neighbour, and *respect* for oneself (*self-esteem*)" (Morals 6:399). There is no obligation to have these moral endowments, Kant writes, precisely because they "lie at the basis of morality, as *subjective* conditions of receptiveness to the concept of duty, not as objective conditions of morality" (Morals 6:399). Not only does self-conceit fail to occupy such a place at the foundation of morality, on Kant's view, but it also constitutes a hindrance to moral development.

22 CJ 5:245.

23 CJ 5:244–245.

24 CJ 5:261.

25   CJ 5:252.

26   CJ 5:252.

27   CJ 5:256.

28   CJ 5:255.

29   CJ 5:253.

30   CJ 5:254.

31   CJ 5:261.

32   CJ 5:261.

33   CJ 5:261.

34   CJ 5:261–262.

35   CJ 5:262.

36   Paul Crowther, who considers sublimity in internal nature to be a variety
       of dynamical sublimity, offers an interpretation of the former that is similar
       in spirit to the present one. He maintains that we may experience sublimity
       "when some affect arises in circumstances that enable us to become more
       generally aware of our moral capacity and its possible employments" (*The
       Kantian Sublime: From Morality to Art* [Oxford: Oxford University Press,
       1989], 117).

37   CJ 5:272. In the third *Critique*, Kant distinguishes affects from passions.
       Affects, he claims, "are related merely to feeling; passions belong to the
       faculty of desire, and are inclinations that hinder or render impossible
       all determinability of the power of choice through principles." Whereas
       Kant holds that affects may be sublime, he holds that "[u]nder no circum-
       stances" can passions be sublime, for the reason that "while the freedom
       of the mind is, no doubt, *impeded* in the case of affects, in passion it is
       abrogated (CJ 5:272n.).

38   CJ 5:276.

39   CJ 5:276.

40   CJ 5:271–272.

41   CJ 5:275.

42   Maladies 2:267.

43   Maladies 2:267.

44   Maladies 2:267. Cf. CJ 5:272.

45   Conflict 7:85.

46   CJ 5:271–272.

47   See also Clewis's examination of some of the potential moral epistemo-
       logical implications of the thesis that enthusiasm is a sublime mental state.
       According to Clewis, Kant holds that enthusiasm functions, for instance,
       as a "morally encouraging sign" and as a means for us to "recognize the
       morally good" (*The Kantian Sublime and the Revelation of Freedom*, 3).

48   CJ 5:272.

49 Anthropology 7:254.

50 Morals 6:408.

51 CJ 5:252–253. Of course, Kant's view is that we can experience not just artifacts, but also natural objects as having internal ends, which is why he also maintains that we cannot expect experiences of pure sublimity in connection with natural objects which "*in their very concept import a determinate end*," including "animals of a recognized natural order" (CJ 5:252–253).

52 Kant's own examples of experiences of sublimity reveal that conceptual understanding will in many cases partly ground the pleasure we feel. We often first need to form representations of objects using sophisticated concepts in order to be able to experience them as sublime. For instance, we need to know what kind of thing we are dealing with in order to be able to represent it as fearful, and, consequently, to be able to experience dynamical sublimity as we engage with it. We need to know, for example, that we are dealing with "[b]old, overhanging ... threatening rocks, thunderclouds piled up the vault of heaven." But making such classifications requires employing sophisticated concepts – including natural kind concepts.

53 CJ 5:253.

54 See Clewis, *The Kantian Sublime and the Revelation of Freedom*, 109.

55 CJ 5:253.

56 CJ 5:270.

57 CJ 5:270.

58 Observations 2:208.

59 See the articulations of Kantian conceptions of artistic sublimity in Crowther, *The Kantian Sublime*, ch. 7, and Clewis, *The Kantian Sublime and the Revelation of Freedom*, 117–125. These constitute novel and interesting developments of Kant's account, and seem to be, in large part, consistent with the remarks on artistic sublimity in the present work. On Crowther's articulation, we are apt to experience sublimity while engaging with art if the work is overwhelming in perceptual scale, overwhelming in personal significance, or overwhelming in its embodiment of a general truth. On Clewis's account, it is possible to experience sublimity in response to vast and powerful human creations, such as skyscrapers.

60 CJ 5:267. Crowther's interpretation of Kant on these points is, broadly speaking, in agreement with the present one. Crowther claims that Kant assumes that "any overcoming of sensibility by reason (in the broad sense of that term) will be of moral significance in so far as it will lead us to take a pleasure in the fact that we are more than creatures of sensibility," and that this will have the effect of rendering us "all the more liable to follow the precepts of moral reason" (*The Kantian Sublime*, 122).

61   Malcolm Budd presents a criticism of the Kantian account of sublimity along these lines. According to Budd, Kant's "identification of pleasure in the sublime as pleasure in the felt realization of our superiority to nature" lacks plausibility, at least if it is supposed to amount to a general explanation of why we feel pleasure while engaging with the kinds of objects under consideration. As Budd puts it, what was very likely a feature of Kant's own experience "is highly likely to be absent from the experience of many, if not most, of us" ("Delight in the Natural World: Kant on the Aesthetic Appreciation of Nature. Part III: The Sublime in Nature," *British Journal of Aesthetics* 38, no. 3 [1998]: 246).

62   CJ 5:244.

6

Choosing Culture Over Happiness

The Ultimate End of Nature

We have seen that Rousseau holds that the pursuit of the pleasures associated with the arts tends to make us worse morally. Kant's view, by contrast, is that, although some pleasures are morally harmful to us, there is no harm in pursuing the pleasures of beauty and sublimity, whether through nature or art. In fact, pursuing these pleasures actually contributes to our moral development. Although Kant and Rousseau disagree over the moral implications of pursuing aesthetic pleasure, they agree on at least one thing: moral development is worth pursuing. Suppose, though, that Kant must now face a different philosopher. This philosopher does not see why it is worth pursuing culture to begin with, given that this involves distancing herself from her inclinations. Can anything be said to such a philosopher to convince her of the error of her ways? Kant, in fact, takes up the task of addressing just such an opponent, most notably in the Appendix to the Critique of Teleological Judgment. Before turning to the Appendix argument, however, it will be worth briefly surveying Kant's articulation, in other works, of several further arguments for this conclusion.

The Possibility of Culture: Pleasure and Moral Development in Kant's Aesthetics,
First Edition. Bradley Murray.

In the *Metaphysics of Morals*, for example, Kant claims that it is a "duty for a man to make his end the perfection belonging to man as such (properly speaking, to humanity)."[1] Here, he takes perfection, generally speaking, to concern "the harmony of a thing's properties with an *end*," and a human being's "natural perfection," specifically, to be bound up with the "*cultivation* of any *capacities* for furthering ends set forth by reason."[2] Thus, on the present conception, pursuing perfection as a human being will go hand in hand with pursuing culture. As it stands, the argument is less than compelling. Even granting this conception of human perfection, the question remains as to why, exactly, we might have a *duty* to pursue our perfection. Kant's answer is simply that this duty exists because the capacity to set such ends for ourselves is what characterizes humanity, and distinguishes human beings from other animals.[3] The reason why such an argument is less than compelling, as it stands, is that it is not at first glance clear why it would follow from the mere fact that one kind of being possesses a capacity not possessed by another kind of being that the first ought to *develop* that capacity.

Next, we find in the *Groundwork* two arguments, which aim to defend not just the claim that we have a duty to pursue culture, but the more specific claim that we have a duty to pursue this even if and when doing so forces us to restrict our pursuit of pleasure. The stages of culture that Kant has in mind in both cases appear to be those of skill and prudence (see Chapter 1), and the arguments take for granted that we will very often need to decide between pursuing culture, on the one hand, and enjoying pleasure, on the other. The case on which Kant focuses is one in which an individual has a talent which, if cultivated, would make him a "human being useful for all sorts of purposes." However, this person's circumstances are comfortable, and he would rather pursue pleasures, such as "idleness, amusement, [and] procreation," than to "trouble himself with enlarging and improving his fortunate natural dispositions."[4]

Each of the two *Groundwork* arguments involves the application of a different formulation of the categorical imperative. Briefly to review what this means for Kant, he holds that, when we carry out particular actions, we do so based on maxims – that is, on subjective principles of volition.[5] Maxims concern particular ends in acting, and the means that we are willing to adopt in order to achieve such ends.[6] For example, the maxim underlying the action of someone who breaks his promises is, perhaps, "I will make a false promise whenever it is convenient to me." Morally evaluating an action is a matter of evaluating the maxim that underlies it in light of the moral law, which Kant maintains finds its expression in the form of a categorical imperative. Thus, the content of one formulation of the categorical imperative – the Formula of Universal Law – is the following: "*I ought never to act except in such a way that I could also will that my maxim should become a universal law.*"[7] To evaluate morally the promise-breaker's action using the Formula of Universal Law, we consider whether he could genuinely will that his maxim should become a universal law. Kant, of course, holds that the promise-breaker cannot genuinely will this insofar as he is rational, since he would recognize that the result would be to render promise-making a completely useless activity. Thus, Kant maintains, such a maxim would "have to destroy itself."[8]

The *Groundwork* arguments for the pursuit of culture over pleasure do not invoke the Formula of Universal Law, but rather two other formulations of the categorical imperative. The first is the Formula of the Law of Nature, which states: "*act as if the maxim of your action were to become by your will a universal law of nature,*"[9] and the second is the Formula of Humanity, which states: "*[s]o act that you use humanity, whether in your own person or in the person of any other, always at the same time as an end, never merely as a means.*"[10] Kant, of course, holds that these two formulations, along with the Formula of Universal Law, are equivalent ways of expressing the moral law.

The Formula of the Law of Nature argument is that the action of someone who chooses to pursue pleasure over culture fails to possess moral worth, since it fails the Formula of the Law of Nature test. Suppose that the maxim that underlies this individual's action is something like the following, which we can call the "maxim of enjoyment": "I will neglect the development of my talents and instead devote my life entirely to idleness and pleasure."[11] The reason why this fails the Formula of the Law of Nature test is not, Kant claims, because we can form no coherent conception of nature in which every human being chooses to pursue pleasure over developing his or her talents. Indeed nature could "always subsist with such a universal law."[12] What is apparently impossible is simply that a rational agent should *will* that anything like the maxim of enjoyment should become a universal law. However, Kant does not explain why it would be impossible for a rational agent to will this, and Kant's opponents – including those who would rather pursue idleness and pleasure than cultivate their talents – would be right to complain that the argument is unpersuasive as it stands.

The Formula of Humanity argument invokes the claim that humanity is an end in itself. An end in itself is something that has unconditional or absolute worth entirely independently of whether it can serve something else as a means. Anything with absolute worth in this sense will be "priceless" and, as such, Kant maintains, will possess dignity. As Kant puts it, "what has a price can be replaced by something else as its *equivalent*; what on the other hand is raised above all price and therefore admits of no equivalent has a dignity."[13] Kant's more general view – which we began to consider in Chapter 5 – is that humanity's dignity inheres in its rational nature and ensuing capacity for morality.[14] To put it briefly, the Formula of Humanity requires that we not use a human being merely as a means, and hence that we act in ways that respect the dignity of human beings. This includes acting in ways that respect one's own dignity.

According to the Formula of Humanity argument, a maxim such as the maxim of enjoyment fails the Formula of Humanity test. Kant reasons, first of all, that we must recognize that there is a distinction between actions which "conflict" with humanity "in our person as an end in itself," actions which preserve our humanity as an end in itself, and actions which "harmonize with" or "further" this end. Our duty, Kant claims, is not simply to act in ways which do not conflict with, or which preserve our humanity as an end in itself, but to act in ways that further our humanity. Next, he suggests that, although neglecting the development of our talents in order to pursue pleasure "might admittedly be consistent with the *preservation* of humanity as an end in itself," it is not consistent "with the *furtherance* of this end."[15]

One reason why Kant might hold that it is only by developing our talents that we further our own humanity is because he believes that, by developing talents relating to skill and prudence, we take important steps towards moralization. But, he might continue, we only respect ourselves as human beings if we aim at furthering our moral nature. This, in turn, is perhaps because our very human dignity arises out of our capacity for morality.[16] Even if something like this is correct, however, it remains a vague proposal. As with the *Metaphysics of Morals* and Formula of Law of Nature arguments, Kant does not explain the key moves that he takes to support the relevant claim, which, in this case, is that there is a connection between humanity's being an end in itself and our having a duty to chose to pursue culture over pleasure. Consequently, it is by no means obvious that either the Formula of Humanity argument, or the first two arguments, ultimately stand a chance of success.

Whereas the *Metaphysics of Morals* and *Groundwork* arguments invoke the notion of duty, the Appendix argument does not directly invoke this notion. Rather, it depends on the claim that pursuing enjoyment at the expense of culture is not compatible with living a worthwhile human life. In fact, Kant raises this possibility as early as the First Moment of the *Critique of Judgment*, where he claims that reason will never accept "that there is any intrinsic worth in the real existence of a man who merely lives for *enjoyment*, however busy he may be in this respect."[17] But it is not until the Appendix that he further develops and defends this possibility by addressing the closely related claim that "[t]he value of life for us, measured simply by *what we enjoy* (by the natural end of the sum of all our inclinations, that is by happiness), is easy to decide. It is less than nothing."[18] The Appendix argument, in outline, is that we have reason to conduct ourselves in ways that contribute to our living worthwhile lives; but only the pursuit of culture, and not the pursuit of happiness or enjoyment, contributes to this end; therefore, we have reason to pursue culture at the expense of happiness.

Kant's defense of the claim that a worthwhile human life is one that is devoted to the pursuit of culture at the expense of happiness seeks first to establish that it is possible, if not necessary, to conceive of humanity as the "ultimate end of nature" (*letzten Zweck der Natur*). Insofar as we conceive of humanity in this way, the argument continues, we are also committed to conceiving of a worthwhile human life as one devoted to the pursuit of culture rather than happiness.

To understand what this means, we must consider Kant's distinction between what he calls "intrinsic" and "extrinsic" or "relative" finality. Recall that finality is the feature that an object may possess of seeming to be related to a maker's concept, "so far as this concept is regarded as the cause of the object (the real ground of its possibility)."[19] To possess finality is to possess the property of seeming to have come into existence through an act of making, or of seeming to be an end, in the object sense of the word.[20] In the case of intrinsic finality, we not only experience the object as an end, in the object sense, but more specifically, as one that has been brought into existence *for its own sake*. In the case of "extrinsic" finality, too, we experience the object as an end; but we experience it as one that has been brought into existence for the sake of *some other* object, rather than for its own sake.[21]

Kant typically equates adopting a perspective of intrinsic finality on an object with considering the object as an "art-product" or artifact – and we have seen that it is possible in his view to consider an object in this way even if it is in fact a natural object.[22] It is common, if not required, he maintains, for biologists to adopt such a perspective when they dissect plants and animals with the aim of investigating their structure and of seeing the "reasons why and the end for which they are provided with such and such parts, why the parts have such and such a position and interconnection, and why the internal form is precisely what it is."[23] Although such things as herbs, plants, and organisms can be considered as things of art, and thus as intrinsically final, they are also paradigm cases of things that can also be considered as extrinsically final.

Generally speaking, Kant claims, insofar as an object can be conceived of as possessing extrinsic finality, it can be conceived of as occupying fundamentally different places in relations of extrinsic finality; when it is possible to think of A as existing for the sake of B, it is typically also possible to think of B as existing for the sake of A.[24] For instance, in constructing one picture of the relations of extrinsic finality in the natural world, we might begin with the question of why members of the vegetable kingdom exist, and answer this by saying that they "exist for the animal kingdom, which is thus provided with the means of sustenance, so that it has been enabled to spread over the face of the earth in such a manifold variety of genera."[25] But we can also construct a different picture by beginning with the question of why herbivorous animals exist, and answering that they exist "for the purpose of checking the profuse growth of the vegetable kingdom by which many species of that kingdom would be choked."[26]

To return to Kant's claim that humanity is the ultimate end of nature, this is, first of all, the claim that humanity is an end, in the object sense. In other words, its coming into existence will have been the desired effect of some agent, and this agent's representation of such an effect preceded its act of bringing humanity into existence. Next, insofar as humanity is the ultimate end of nature, it will be the end *for the sake of which* everything else in nature exists as a means. Humanity will have a special status within the natural world, with everything else in nature serving as a means to its flourishing.[27]

As will become clearer shortly, Kant does not maintain that we could ever prove that humanity is the ultimate end of nature. But he does suggest one way in which we might be led to form such a picture of the world, and this is by recognizing that human beings seem to be unique within the natural world because we possess rationality. As Kant puts it, we might think of the human being as "the one and only being upon [the earth] that is able to form a conception of ends, and from an aggregate of things purposively fashioned to construct by the aid of his reason a system of ends."[28] This uniqueness could, in turn, potentially be used to justify the claim that humanity enjoys a special status in nature.

The Liberation of the Will

Simply supposing for now that humanity is the ultimate end of nature, it still remains to be seen why this might entail that we have reason to make the pursuit of culture a central aim of our lives.

The Appendix argument depends on an implicit assumption, namely, that there is a connection between the worth of a human life and the purpose of a human life. We can better understand why Kant might have accepted such an assumption if we consider as an analogy the case of an artifact's goodness. For example, a watch has a purpose or function, namely, to enable its users to keep track of the time of day. Correspondingly, at least one aspect of the worth or value of the watch will be connected with how well it fulfills the purpose of a watch. A good watch successfully performs this function, and a poor watch fails to perform it. Just as the watch is an end whose worth is correlated with the purpose it is to fulfill, so, we can say, a human being is an end whose worth is correlated with the purpose he or she is to fulfill.[29]

Kant's thought is that it is possible to arrive at a conception of the purpose of human beings by, first, supposing that nature itself is striving to enable us to realize our purpose, and, second, attempting to form an interpretation of nature which will shed light on its underlying intentions for us. Thus, Kant suggests, we are to look for "the end in man, and the end which, as such, is intended to be promoted by means of his connection with nature."[30] And Kant's argument, in outline, is that, if we are presented with a choice between interpreting nature as intending to promote our efforts at achieving happiness, on the one hand, and interpreting it as intending to promote our efforts at achieving culture, on the other hand, it will be most appropriate to choose the latter interpretation. As Kant puts the point, "it is only culture that can be the ultimate end which we have cause to attribute to nature in respect of the human race."[31] But given the assumption that there is a connection between the purpose and worth of a human life, we will then be able to say that the worth of a human life is greater to the extent that the individual achieves his or her culture.

In exploring the first of the two interpretations of nature just mentioned, the interpretation according to which nature's intention is to enable us to achieve happiness, Kant invokes a notion of happiness (*Glückseligkeit*) as the "natural end of the sum of all our inclinations."[32] Because of the nature of happiness, Kant maintains, we face certain practical difficulties if we set out to attain it. Happiness is "a mere *idea* of a state," and one that does not specify with any precision what it would be for such a state to obtain.[33] It is because happiness is "such an indeterminate concept" that an individual who wishes to achieve it "can still never say determinately and consistently with himself what he really wishes and wills." One cause of the difficulty in specifying what will make us happy is that, no matter how insightful we are, we will not be in a position to foresee all the consequences of getting what we presently think will make us happy. For example, Kant claims, if we will riches and end up attaining this, our lives could be characterized by unexpected feelings of anxiety and envy. If we will knowledge and insight, we could end up seeing more keenly the ills in the world that we currently do not notice. If we will a long life, this could end up being filled with misery; and if we will health, the absence of bodily discomfort could lead us to take up "excesses" that we might otherwise avoid.[34]

Because it is so difficult for us to specify what our happiness might involve, moreover, Kant holds that we will often be tempted to choose to act to bring about immediate enjoyment. For example, he claims, it might initially seem rational for someone suffering from gout to choose not to enjoy what he likes in the present because of an expectation of greater happiness that lies in health. However, the matter is not as straightforward as it might seem; it could actually be rational for the gout sufferer to act to satisfy a "single inclination, determinate both as to what it promises and as to the time within which it can be satisfied," precisely because he recognizes that his expectation of future happiness that lies in good health could be "groundless."[35]

Although Kant maintains that we face practical obstacles to making happiness our aim, it is not primarily on the basis of the existence of such obstacles that he suggests that we interpret nature as intending to promote our culture rather than our happiness. His argument depends, instead, on an interpretation of nature as itself being set up in order to ensure our misery in the long term. Thus, Kant claims that it can appear as if "external nature is far from having made a particular favourite of man or from having preferred him to all other animals as the object of its beneficence," since we see that "in its destructive operations – plague, famine, flood, cold, attacks from animals great and small, and all such things – it has as little spared him as any other animal."[36] Kant makes a similar point in the *Idea for a Universal History*, where he claims that it can seem to have "pleased nature" to exercise frugality in regard to our happiness.[37] Not only, Kant continues, can external nature be interpreted as undermining any hope of long-term happiness, but our internal natures are also susceptible to such an interpretation. Through his "inner *natural tendencies*," Kant claims, humankind faces

> further misfortunes of his own invention, and reduces other members of his species, through the oppression of lordly power, the barbarism of wars, and the like, to such misery, while he himself does all he can to work ruin to his race, that, even with the utmost goodwill on the part of external nature, its end, supposing it were directed to the happiness of our species, would never be attained in a system of terrestrial nature, because our own nature is not capable of it.[38]

Once we come to recognize the destructiveness of nature, in both its external and internal forms, Kant claims, it is appropriate that we interpret it as aiming, specifically, to promote our "negative culture" or "culture of discipline." As mentioned in Chapter 1, Kant takes this kind of culture to function to remove obstacles to "the *will* in its determination and choice of its ends,"[39] with the net result of bringing about the "liberation of the will from the despotism of desires whereby, in our attachment to certain natural things, we are rendered incapable of exercising a choice of our own."[40] The kinds of obstacles that negative culture can remove, then, will be those that come from our own inclinations. The inclinations, as Kant has put it, constitute "a great impediment to the development of our humanity," even if they may be "very purposively adapted to the performance of our essential functions as an animal species."[41]

Kant's thought, then, is that to recognize nature as impeding us in our pursuit of happiness is to recognize it as serving to promote our negative culture. That is, nature is, as it were, exercising a form of "tough love," aiming to teach us to learn to do without the satisfaction of our inclinations.

By the Constitution of Our Understanding

Assuming, as we are for the time being, that it does make sense to talk of interpreting nature to begin with, two initial difficulties present themselves concerning the proposed interpretation itself. The first is that Kant does not defend his suggestion that, when it comes to interpretations of nature, the only live options are those according to which it aims to promote our happiness or our culture. But given that there are surely other possible interpretations, we are owed such a defense.

The second difficulty is simply that what Kant takes to constitute the evidence supporting the interpretation that nature wishes to impede our pursuit of happiness – evidence in the form of events such as natural disasters – does not in itself make such an interpretation necessary. For all we know, things might have been much worse for humanity than they actually are, and nature could be doing all that it can to promote our happiness. It is just that there are limitations to what it can do. The natural world that we inhabit could, in fact, be the one that is more conducive to human happiness than any other possible natural world.[42] On such an interpretation, we could, after all, say that a human life possesses worth to the extent that it is lived primarily in pursuit of happiness. While there may be some room for doubt in any interpretation – even in more straightforward cases involving ordinary human speech and artifacts – the issue here does not depend on general difficulties relating to interpretation, as such. Rather, the difficulty seems to be that we have particularly little to go on in attempting to interpret nature.

Even leaving these interpretive issues aside, however, there is another aspect of the Appendix argument that is surprising to many of Kant's readers. This is his suggestion that it can be appropriate to think of humanity as the ultimate end of nature to begin with. In fact, although it might initially seem as if Kant takes quite literally the claim that humanity is the ultimate end of nature, he is clear in the Appendix that he is not advancing such a claim. For he takes himself to have shown only that "looking to principles of reason, there is ample ground – for the reflective, though not of course for the determinant, judgement – to make us estimate man as not merely a physical end, such as all organized beings are, but as the being upon this earth who is the *ultimate end* of nature."[43]

In clarifying that he is speaking at the level of reflective rather than determinant judgment, Kant is alluding to his view that it is often useful and justified for us to adopt points of view on the world that we cannot, strictly speaking, know to correspond to the way the world actually is. Kant's claims concerning reflective judgment in the third *Critique* mirror those concerning what, in the first *Critique*, he refers to as the "regulative use of reason" or the application of "regulative ideas." An idea, Kant maintains, is something that cannot be borrowed from the senses, and, moreover, it concerns matters that cannot be captured by the concepts of the understanding.[44] To say that an idea is "regulative" is to say that it merely serves as a kind of "rule of pure reason," directing reason to proceed in certain directions.[45] The idea of God, for example, is on Kant's view an idea of pure reason, in the sense that, although we "do not have the least reason to assume absolutely" that God exists, reason nonetheless "bids us consider every connection in the world according to principles of a systematic unity, hence *as if* they had all arisen from one single all-encompassing being, as supreme and all-sufficient cause."[46] Our proceeding "as if" God were the creator of the universe amounts to our employing the idea of God regulatively.

We find in Kant two distinct strategies for addressing difficult questions surrounding the justification of regulative uses of reason. One is to suggest that, owing to the nature of reason, we cannot avoid employing it in this way. But, this line of thinking continues, it would be inappropriate to withhold justification from uses of reason that are inevitable. Along these lines, Kant claims, for instance, that principles of finality in nature assert only that "by the constitution of our understanding and our reason we are unable to conceive the origin in the case of beings of this kind otherwise than in the light of final causes."[47] When it comes, specifically, to our experiencing organisms as if they were designed, Kant's view is that human reason "could never discover a particle of foundation for what constitutes the specific character of a physical end" if it did not permit itself to seek out explanations that invoke the notion of design.[48] In fact, Kant suggests, "[t]he very notion that they are organized things is itself impossible unless we associate with it the notion of a production by design."[49] Thus, Kant's view is that when we are dealing with organized natural products, "we cannot get rid of the necessity of adopting the conception of a design as basal"; we must assume "a cause working designedly, and, consequently, a being whose productivity is analogous to the causality of an understanding."[50]

Kant's second strategy for addressing questions relating to the justification of regulative uses of reason emerges most clearly in his discussion of regulative ideas in the first *Critique*. For example, he claims that the principle that God is responsible for designing the world "opens up for our reason, as applied to the field of experience, entirely new prospects for connecting up things in the world in accordance with teleological laws," which in turn can be useful to us as we seek to make new discoveries. But, Kant continues, there is no harm in making such a supposition as long as we do not forget that we may only do so regulatively. For even if we are in error, no harm is done: "nothing more can follow from it in any case than that where we expected a teleological connection (*nexus finalis*), a merely mechanical or physical one (*nexus effectivus*) is to be found."[51]

Here, Kant is invoking what might be called a "pragmatic justification" principle.[52] That is, to be justified in making a teleological attribution to nature, we must be acting in pursuit of goals and interests that are bound up with our rational drive for unified knowledge or moral coherence.[53] In other words, making such an attribution must help us to extend our knowledge or further our moral vocation, by enabling us to form a more systematic conception of the world than we otherwise could do. Given this principle, a biologist, for example, would be justified in adopting a teleological principle in investigating nature insofar as this makes possible further scientific discoveries.

By keeping in mind Kant's notion of a regulative use of reason as we approach the Appendix argument, we see how Kant is able to forestall the objection that, given that we cannot know humanity to be the ultimate end of nature, and for that matter cannot know nature to have any intentions with respect to humanity, we are in no position to make use of such claims in order to articulate a conception of the worth of a human life. The argument does not depend on our having any such knowledge, and this is precisely because Kant is speaking merely at the level of the regulative rather than constitutive use of reason, or, in other words, at the level of reflective rather than determinant judgment.

But, by speaking at this level, the argument will face a new difficulty, which can be captured in the form of a dilemma. The underlying issue is whether the claim is that we *must*, or simply that we *may*, employ reason regulatively in order to think of humanity as the ultimate end of nature.

Suppose, on the one hand, that the claim is that we must think this way. We actually do have some reason to think that Kant accepts this claim, for in Section 21 of the Appendix, immediately after he considers what it would be for humanity to be the ultimate end of nature, he refers to principles of teleological generation of organic natural beings, which he takes to be principles that are properly employed only regulatively. Even so, these are principles according to which "by the constitution of our understanding and our reason we are unable to conceive the origin in the case of beings of this kind otherwise than in the light of final causes."[54] It is possible that Kant's discussing the claim that humanity is the ultimate end of nature alongside his discussion of the employment of principles of teleological generation in this way indicates that he takes the former, like the latter, to be connected with necessary operations of reason. If this is Kant's view, then, on the surface at least, it lacks plausibility. For there are doubtless many individuals who will deny that the thought that humanity is the ultimate end of nature – much less that, as such, nature has a hidden plan for humanity – has ever crossed their minds. It will be difficult for Kant plausibly to maintain the necessity of this way of thinking in the face of the widespread denials he is bound to face.

The second alternative is that Kant's underlying view is merely that we may think of humanity as the ultimate end of nature. If this is his view, then we can see potential analogies with at least one way of characterizing the biologist's stance towards an organism. While doing biology, the biologist proceeds as if the organism had an internal end. But, at other times, the biologist is presumably able to relinquish this perspective. As mentioned, his or her teleological stance towards the organism is justified, if at all, in Kant's view, by a pragmatic justification principle. Similarly, Kant's view might be that someone who takes seriously the thought that humanity is the ultimate end of nature and behaves as if it is, may be justified by a pragmatic justification principle. This, perhaps, is the principle that making such teleological attributions to nature is justified if, say, doing so furthers the goals and interests of morality. And, indeed, Kant could maintain that the interests of morality are served by our adopting such a perspective on humanity's place in nature, precisely because our doing so motivates us to pursue culture – whose end, of course, is moralization.

Although this strategy enjoys some plausibility, it yields a version of the Appendix argument that will have little force against many of Kant's opponents. Specifically, it will lack force against those who maintain that pursuing happiness is part of a worthwhile life, and who also happen not to be drawn to the thought that humanity is the ultimate end of nature. Kant could perhaps reply that such individuals *ought* to take this thought on board – because, say, they ought to use their reason regulatively in ways that further the ends of morality. Consequently, these individuals could perhaps in some way be criticized for not doing so. But this is a stronger claim than Kant, in fact, argues for, and it is not obvious how such an argument could plausibly be developed and defended.

The Appendix argument, then, faces at least two sorts of difficulties: those relating to the interpretation of nature, and those relating to the claim that we are to think regulatively of humanity as the ultimate end of nature. In the end, the argument cannot be said to be very compelling. The bottom line is that Kant does not establish in a way that can be expected to satisfy his opponents that we have reason to pursue culture, or that we have reason to do so at the expense of pursuing pleasure or happiness. The failure of the Appendix argument – and, indeed of the *Metaphysics of Morals* and *Groundwork* arguments – does not, however, detract from the interest or importance of the ethical underpinnings of Kant's aesthetics. Namely, it does not detract from the fact that it is able to articulate a plausible account of the connections between aesthetic pleasure and moral development that anyone who does, in fact, have a concern to pursue culture has reason to take seriously. This is not only intrinsically important, but also important when it comes to responding to anti-aesthetic arguments, such as Rousseau's, that are grounded in ethical concerns.

Notes

1   Morals 6:386–387.
2   Morals 6:391. Cf. Morals 6:386–387; Morals 6:444.
3   Morals 6:392.
4   Groundwork 4:423.
5   Groundwork 4:402n.
6   See Allen Wood, *Kant's Ethical Thought* (Cambridge: Cambridge University Press), 78.
7   Groundwork 4:402.
8   Groundwork 4:403.
9   Groundwork 4:421.
10 Groundwork 4:429.
11 See Wood, *Kant's Ethical Thought*, 90.
12 Groundwork 4:423.
13 Groundwork 4:434.
14 Groundwork 4:435.
15 Groundwork 4:430.
16 The claim that human beings possess the capacity for morality insofar as we possess dignity does not entail that human beings who do not, for whatever reason, exercise this capacity lack dignity, and hence that they lack worth and need not be treated as full-fledged persons. One distinguishing feature of Kantian ethics is that it resists introducing comparisons having to do with the basic worth of individuals. All human beings – and indeed all possible rational agents – are claimed to be ends in themselves and to possess dignity. See Wood, *Kant's Ethical Thought*, 138; Elizabeth Anderson, "Emotions in Kant's Later Moral Philosophy: Honour and the Phenomenology of Moral Value," in *Kant's Ethics of Virtue*, ed. Monika Betzler (Berlin: Walter de Gruyter, 2008), 139; and Stephen Darwall, "Kant on Respect, Dignity, and the Duty of Respect," in *Kant's Ethics of Virtue*, ed. Monika Betzler (Berlin: Walter de Gruyter, 2008), 175–200.
17 CJ 5:208–209.
18 CJ 5:434n.
19 CJ 5:220.
20 See Chapter 3.
21 Kant distinguishes between cases in which a human being's ends are at issue, and those in which another animal's ends are at issue. He describes extrinsic finality in the former case as "utility" and in the latter case as "adaptability" (CJ 5:367).
22 CJ 5:367.
23 CJ 5:376.

24   CJ 5:425.

25   CJ 5:426.

26   CJ 5:427.

27   Kant's claim that humanity is the ultimate end of nature is distinct from another claim that he also endorses, namely that humanity is the "final end" (*Endzweck*) of nature. A final end, Kant writes, "must be presupposed as that in relation to which the contemplation of the world may itself possess a worth," and it is "only as a moral being that man can be a final end of creation" (CJ 5:442–443). As Paul Guyer points out, whereas the former claim is value neutral, the latter is value-positive (*Kant's System of Nature and Freedom: Selected Essays* [Oxford: Clarendon Press, 2005], 331). Kant's argument for the claim that humanity is the final end of nature interacts with his argument for the claim that humanity is the ultimate end of nature. Specifically, the former seems to presuppose the latter. The present focus is on the latter, more modest and less controversial claim. For more on the interaction between these claims, see Guyer, *Kant's System of Nature and Freedom*, chs. 12 and 13, and Thomas Pogge, "Kant on Ends and the Meaning of Life," in *Reclaiming the History of Ethics: Essays for John Rawls*, ed. Andrews Reath, Barbara Herman, and Christine M. Korsgaard (Cambridge: Cambridge University Press, 1997), 361–387.

28   CJ 5:427.

29   Since Kant's view is that it is not possible to compare the worth of persons, as such, we can take it that what is in question here is, broadly speaking, the worth of what might be called an individual's "way of life."

30   CJ 5:429.

31   CJ 5:431.

32   CJ 5:434n. This is consistent with his conception, in the *Groundwork*, of happiness as the idea in which "all inclinations unite in one sum" (Groundwork 4:399).

33   CJ 5:430. Cf. Groundwork 4:399.

34   Groundwork 4:418.

35   Groundwork 4:399.

36   CJ 5:430.

37   Idea 8:19. Similarly, Kant claims in the Groundwork that "in a being that has reason and a will, if the proper end of nature were its preservation, its welfare, in a word its happiness, then nature would have hit upon a very bad arrangement in selecting the reason of the creature to carry out this purpose" (Groundwork 4:395).

38   CJ 5:430.

39   CJ 5:431.

40   CJ 5:432.

41 CJ 5:433.
42 Even Kant appears to operate with a conception of happiness that is not bound up with the short-term satisfaction of inclinations. Instead, this longer-term conception of happiness is bound up with the concept of the highest good (as in CPrR 5:130–131). See Guyer, *Kant's System of Nature and Freedom*, 335.
43 CJ 5:429.
44 CPR A313/B370.
45 CPR A509/B537.
46 CPR A686/B714.
47 CJ 5:429.
48 CJ 5:388.
49 CJ 5:398.
50 CJ 5:397–398.
51 CPR A687/B715.
52 For similar interpretations, see John McFarland, *Kant's Concept of Teleology* (Edinburgh: University of Edinburgh Press, 1970), 86, and Andrew Chignell, "Kant's Concepts of Justification," *Noûs* 41, no. 1 (2007): 50. Pogge emphasizes the "heuristic" function of such attributions ("Kant on Ends and the Meaning of Life," 371), as does Henry Allison, "Teleology and History in Kant: The Critical Foundations of Kant's Philosophy of History," in *Kant's Idea for a Universal History with a Cosmopolitan Aim*, ed. Amélie Oksenberg Rorty and James Schmidt (Cambridge: Cambridge University Press, 2009), 36.
53 Chignell, "Kant's Concepts of Justification," 53.
54 CJ 5:429.

7

Conclusion

Two general issues have been lingering over the preceding examination of Kant's aesthetics. The first is the issue of what, if any, moral significance a Kantian aesthetic theory might assign to the experience of ugliness. The second has to do with the unmistakably empirical flavor of the side of Kant's aesthetics on which we have been focusing. We may feel compelled to ask what, if any, basis there might be for the claims about human moral development on which the account relies, and perhaps also whether there is reason to take such an account seriously given that there is another side of Kant's aesthetics which can appear, at first, at any rate, not to rest on an empirical foundation. This concluding chapter will address these issues in turn.

In the preceding chapters, we have focused exclusively on the moral significance of experiences of aesthetic *pleasure*. It is true that we have examined what Kant considers to be the "negative" aesthetic pleasure of sublimity. But even though sublimity has a displeasurable aspect – owing to the fact that it incorporates an experience of contra-finality – it remains on Kant's view a pleasurable experience, overall. What we have not considered, specifically, is the experience of ugliness, which, unlike the experiences of beauty and sublimity, will be characterized mostly, if not wholly by displeasure. Of course, there is a reason why we have

The Possibility of Culture: Pleasure and Moral Development in Kant's Aesthetics,
First Edition. Bradley Murray.
© 2015 John Wiley & Sons, Inc. Published 2015 by John Wiley & Sons, Inc.

focused on aesthetic pleasure: we have wanted to see how Kant's aesthetics can contribute to a dialogue with those who claim that the pursuit of the pleasures of beauty and sublimity is ethically problematic. The arguments that we have been considering have aimed precisely to establish that the pursuit of such pleasures promote our capacity to act effectively as moral agents.

Kant, famously, has very little to say about ugliness as he develops his aesthetic theory. This can seem surprising: given that it is plausible to think of ugliness as the opposite of beauty, it would seem to make sense for a theory of beauty to set out to offer an explanation that accounts in some way for the former.[1] One reason why Kant neglects ugliness might be that aspects of his aesthetic theory could entail that experiences of ugliness are not possible. More will be said about this possibility shortly, but, briefly put for now, Kant's view may turn out to be that the "harmony" of the cognitive faculties that he takes to be a necessary condition of the experience of objects in general may at the same time be sufficient for having experiences of beauty. If so, this would seem to entail that *any* experience of an object could be an experience of beauty. It would not be initially obvious where experiences of ugliness might fit into Kantian aesthetics.[2] Having said this, it is clear that Kant does believe that there is such a thing as aesthetic displeasure. In the unpublished first introduction to the third *Critique*, for instance, he describes an aesthetic judgment as one "whose determining ground lies in a sensation that is immediately connected with the feeling of pleasure and *displeasure* [emphasis added]."[3] And in the Fourth Moment, Kant claims that judgments of taste "must have a subjective principle, and one which determines what pleases or *displeases*, by means of feeling only and not through concepts, but yet with universal validity [emphasis added]."[4]

Supposing for the sake of argument that Kant's aesthetic theory ultimately does have the capacity fully to explain ugliness, we can ask a particularly relevant question in the context of the present study: if the pursuit of experiences of aesthetic pleasure can promote our moral development, what might be the moral implications of the pursuit of aesthetic displeasure?

There is only space to begin to answer this question here, but we can make such a beginning by considering, in turn, the two main arguments on which we have been focusing. The argument on which we focused in Chapter 3 depended on the claim that aesthetic pleasure is unique in being both pleasing and disinterested, or disconnected from various desires we might have in relation to the sensible object with which we are engaging. Because it is disconnected from these desires, pursuing aesthetic pleasure affords us opportunities to engage in a kind of practice that can teach us to resist sensible inclinations in the pursuit of moral ends. If aesthetic displeasure is also disconnected from our desires in the relevant way, might pursuing it also contribute to our moral development? The answer, it seems, is that it will not. For we can expect that we will typically lack a desire for objects that we find displeasing to begin with. Thus, in the case of aesthetic displeasure, instead of being in the position of experiencing *pleasure without desire*, we are in the position of experiencing *displeasure without desire*. And there is no reason, at first glance, to think that the pursuit of experiences with such a feature would teach us anything of consequence to our moral development. Of course, we might add, there is also no reason to think that the pursuit of experiences with this feature would have a negative effect on our moral development, either – we might expect that the effect would be neutral.

However, things are perhaps different when we turn from the argument starting from the disinterestedness of aesthetic pleasure to the argument starting from the connection between aesthetic pleasure and morally relevant emotions. In the case of beauty, this argument depended on the claim that there is a connection between beauty and love, via the emotion gratitude. In the Appendix to the Critique of Teleological Judgment, Kant considered the case of an individual "amid beautiful surroundings ... in calm and serene enjoyment of his existence [who] feels within him a need – a need of being grateful for it to someone."[5] In reconstructing Kant's view, we suggested that pursuing experiences of beauty affords us opportunities to experience gratitude, which in turn plays a role in the development of our capacity to experience love. The latter is relevant to our moral development since it helps us to adopt an impartial stance and to resist inclinations when needed.

If beauty is closely connected with gratitude and love, then perhaps ugliness could be closely connected with ingratitude and hate. Perhaps someone who undergoes an experience of ugliness can be expected to feel an anxious displeasure in his existence, and to feel a need of expressing ingratitude concerning his lot to someone.[6] Just supposing that there is such a connection between ugliness and ingratitude, we might expect this to correspond to certain consequences when it comes to the pursuit of moral development. First, in the *Metaphysics of Morals*, Kant describes "ingratitude proper" as involving "all-out hatred of one's benefactor."[7] Ingratitude, Kant adds, "stands love of human beings on its head."[8] But if increasing our capacity for love of other human beings serves to enable us to resist our inclinations when doing so is morally necessary, then increasing our feelings of hate could, by contrast, serve to weaken our capacity to resist inclinations. It may do this by serving to isolate us from others, inculcating in us what Kant describes as "separatist misanthropy."[9] Instead of becoming more impartial, as we would in becoming better able to love, the pursuit of experiences of ugliness may lead us to become more self-centered. It is, as mentioned, beyond the scope of the present study to pursue these issues fully here. But it seems at first glance, at least, that we have reason to suspect that the pursuit of ugliness could on an elaboration of Kant's view turn out to be detrimental to our moral development.

Turning to the second, and final issue, it is clear that, as it has been developed in the preceding chapters, Kant's aesthetics certainly cannot be said to be wholly *a priori*. The explanation of the moral significance of the pursuit of aesthetic pleasure has depended on elements of Kant's account of culture, which in turn rests on theses concerning what human beings tend to be like – theses concerning our capacities and standard processes of development. The claims that Kant invokes tend to be empirical claims of a specific sort – they are, namely, claims that emerge primarily from what he calls "pragmatic anthropology."

In the Preface to *Anthropology from a Pragmatic Point of View*, Kant explains that he takes anthropology in general to amount to a "doctrine of the knowledge of the human being, systematically formulated." Anthropology, he claims, can be approached either from a physiological point of view or from a pragmatic point of view. The former makes it an investigation of what "*nature* makes of the human being," whereas the latter makes it an investigation of what "*he* as a free-acting being makes of himself, or can and should make of himself."[10] Pragmatic anthropology proceeds as a discipline by taking up the human perspective, rather than merely by observing human behavior, as it were, from the outside. In engaging in pragmatic anthropology, it will not do merely "to *know* the world" (*die Welt kennen*), but it is instead necessary "to *have* the world" (*die Welt haben*).[11] Kant elucidates this distinction using an analogy of a play: knowing the world, he claims, is akin to merely understanding the play, whereas having the world is akin to *participating* in the play. The methods of pragmatic anthropological investigation must be suited to the nature of the discipline, and will include broadening one's under-standing of human nature through travel or reading travel books, as well as interaction with others who live locally. Although they do not rise to the level of primary sources for pragmatic anthropological investigation, Kant claims that works of world history, biographies, plays, and novels can be of assistance. Novels and plays can serve as useful tools for the pragmatic anthropologist since, however exaggerated the characters may be, they "must have been taken from the observation of the real actions of human beings" and must therefore "correspond to human nature in kind."[12]

Pragmatic anthropological investigation so conceived faces certain obstacles which require us to temper the level of certainty that we attri-bute to its results. Among the most significant obstacles, Kant holds, are those that result from the tendency of human beings to dissemble and dissimulate – both in relation to others and to themselves. When we notice that we are being observed by another who is trying to study us, we may become self-conscious and unable to show ourselves as we really are. Moreover, if we are attempting to study ourselves, we may find it easiest to do so when we are in a contemplative rather than agitated state; but this can impose a profound limitation on self-observation, since we may be exhibiting our nature most clearly exactly at those times when calm contemplation is not possible.

In spite of the obstacles it faces, Kant maintains that pragmatic anthropology remains a valuable source of knowledge, given the unique way in which it is able to make sense of the human point of view. And it is plausible to think of Kant's account of culture as emerging out of an understanding of human nature that will have emerged from his pursuit of the kinds of inquiries that he takes to characterize pragmatic anthropology. It is because he begins with an account of what it is like to be a human being that he is able to venture a proposal as to the stages of our development and the obstacles that we face along the way.

Some might object that Kant should not be in the business of import-ing empirical claims into aesthetic theory. Beneath such an objection is perhaps the more general belief that philosophical investigations should be kept distinct from empirical investigations. Those who put forward such an objection may, moreover, take issue with the nonstandard way in which we have pursued Kant's aesthetics. As alluded to briefly in this book's introduction, it is common to emphasize in accounts of Kantian aesthetics Kant's approach to the issue of the justification of aesthetic judgments, and specifically the "deduction" that is at the centre of this approach. If the aspects of Kant's aesthetic theory that are concerned with the justification of aesthetic judgment do not depend on empirical claims, our opponent might suggest, then we have reason to pursue those aspects, and to ignore the aspects that do depend on such claims – including Kant's view of the connection between aesthetic pleasure and moral development.

Such objections are not compelling. First, it would be a mistake to begin from the assumption that nothing fruitful can emerge from a philosophical investigation that depends on empirical claims. But more importantly, at least when it comes to deciding how best to approach Kant's aesthetics, it is doubtful that the side of his theory that primarily concerns the justification of aesthetic judgment rests purely on *a priori* claims. To better see why, it will help briefly to review Kant's aesthetics insofar as it presents an account of aesthetic justification.

Recall that Hume, in his essay "Of the Standard of Taste," took on a problem that seems to arise on the assumption that aesthetic judgments are based on subjective experiences of pleasure and that the quality of beauty is not strictly speaking a quality of objects.[13] When we make such assumptions, we find it difficult to explain how there could be anything approaching a standard of taste. While he endorsed the subjectivity of taste, Hume held that we are deeply committed to the existence of a standard of taste. Kant shares Hume's starting point, and approaches the problem of aesthetic justification by seeking to offer a deduction of aesthetic judgments.

Kant explains why he thinks that a deduction of judgments of taste is necessary in Section 30 of the third *Critique* – which is the deduction's official beginning.[14] He explains that "the claim of an aesthetic judgement to universal validity for every Subject, being a judgement which must rely on some *a priori* principle, stands in need of a Deduction (i.e. a derivation of its title)."[15] The need for a deduction, then, stems from at least one feature of the underlying logical form of judgments of taste themselves – namely, what Kant calls their "universality." Unlike a judgment that an object is agreeable, which Kant takes merely to make a claim concerning our own personal preferences, a judgment of beauty or sublimity makes a "claim to validity for all men." It would be "ridiculous," according to Kant, "if any one who plumed himself on his taste were to think of justifying himself by saying: This object (the building we see, the dress that person has on, the concert we hear, the poem submitted to our criticism) is beautiful *for me*."[16] Kant continues:

> For if it merely pleases *him*, he must not call it *beautiful*. Many things may for him possess charm and agreeableness – no one cares about that; but when he puts a thing on a pedestal and calls it beautiful, he demands the same delight from others. He judges not merely for himself, but for all men, and then speaks of beauty as if it were a property of things. Thus he says the *thing* is beautiful; and it is not as if he counted on others agreeing in his judgement of liking owing to his having found them in such agreement on a number of occasions, but he *demands* this agreement of them. He blames them if they judge differently, and denies them taste, which he still requires of them as something they ought to have; and to this extent it is not open to men to say: Every one has his own taste. This would be equivalent to saying that there is no such thing at all as taste, i.e. no aesthetic judgement capable of making a rightful claim upon the assent of all men.[17]

It is because an implied claim to universality is part of a judgment of taste that, in Kant's view, "something must lie at its basis as its *a priori* principle" if we are to be in any way justified in making such a judgment.[18] Kant's reasoning here is that the claim that everyone else should approve of a given object is not a claim that could be justified on empirical grounds. It cannot be justified by counting up occasions on which people have actually agreed that the object is beautiful. Instead, it is a claim whose justification seems to be independent of experience; it is an *a priori* claim, and Kant's general view is that *a priori* claims can only be justified if they are grounded in *a priori* principles.

The deduction of judgments of taste, then, seeks to articulate the relevant *a priori* principle and to demonstrate that this principle is in some sense "valid." Kant presents the official version of the Deduction in a single paragraph in Section 38:

> Admitting that in a pure judgement of taste the delight in the object is connected with the mere estimate of its form, then what we feel to be

associated in the mind with the representation of the object is nothing else than its subjective finality for judgement. Since, now, in respect of the formal rules of estimating, apart from all matter (whether sensation or concept), judgement can only be directed to the subjective conditions of its employment in general, (which is not restricted to the particular mode of sense nor to a particular concept of the understanding) and so can only be directed to that subjective factor which we may presuppose in all men (as requisite for a possible experience generally), it follows that the accordance of a representation with these conditions of the judgement admit of being assumed valid *a priori* for every one. In other words, we are warranted in exacting from every one the pleasure or subjective finality of the representation in respect of the relation of the cognitive faculties engaged in the estimate of a sensible object in general."[19]

What emerges beneath the technical detail of this passage is the view that the sought after *a priori* principle makes reference to a "subjective factor" which we may presuppose in every other experiencing subject – and, on a plausible reading, this subjective factor is bound up with the operation of our cognitive faculties. Thus, the *a priori* principle in question is that "the subjective conditions of this faculty of aesthetic judgement are identical in all human beings in what concerns the relation of the cognitive faculties, there brought into action, with a view to a cognition in general."[20] A fuller explanation – which there is not space to pursue here – would likely need to invoke Kant's account of the so-called "harmony" of the cognitive faculties, which he takes to ground both the possibility of experience in general and the possibility of experiences of beauty and sublimity, in particular. In Kant's words, the pleasure felt in an experience of beauty

> must of necessity depend for every one upon the same conditions, seeing that they are the subjective conditions of the possibility of a cognition in general, and the proportion of these cognitive faculties which is requisite for taste is requisite also for ordinary sound understanding, the presence of which we are entitled to presuppose in every one.[21]

One cause for concern at this point is that Kant's account could entail that everything is beautiful. As already mentioned, if the harmony of the cognitive faculties is a necessary condition of the experience of objects in general, but it is at the same time sufficient for having experiences of beauty, then it seems at first glance to follow that *any* experience of an object could be an experience of beauty. Some commentators are willing to attribute such a view to Kant.[22] Those who are not willing to do so, on the other hand, may be forced into taking quite literally his theory of the harmony of the faculties, and appealing to the notion of their "proportionate accord." The idea would be that beautiful objects are those that occasion a special or maximal attunement that everyday objects do not occasion.[23] While this is certainly a possible move that one might make, the theory of the harmony of the faculties is controversial, and it is not obvious that it will ultimately be desirable to place this much weight on it.

Another potential difficulty with Kant's attempted deduction is that, even supposing that the same subjective factor is the ground both of judgments of taste and of experience, more generally, it is still not clear that this is a very substantial result if our aim is to establish that we are justified in particular cases of aesthetic judgment. While Kant does not necessarily take this to be a difficulty, some of his commentators do.[24] From Kant's point of view, at any rate, the fact that we might make mistakes in any given case of aesthetic judgment – specifically, when our judgment is not "pure" and is mixed with "concepts of the Object or sensations as determining grounds" – is not inherently problematic. Rather, it "only touches the incorrect application to a particular case of the right which a law gives us, and does not do away with the right generally."[25]

Even putting these two potential difficulties aside, however, matters quickly become more complicated. For Kant holds that claims of taste imply not just universality, in the sense of an expectation that everyone else will share our pleasure, but also a *demand* that everyone else share this pleasure. That is, in judging something to be beautiful or sublime, we apparently imply that everyone else ought to agree with us. As Kant puts it, the feeling in the judgment of taste is "exacted from every one as a sort of duty."[26] But, whatever else it might establish, it does not seem that the deduction as presented up to Section 39 establishes that such a demand could be legitimate. Kant himself seems to be of this opinion, since he returns later to the issue of the demand implied in judgments of taste in the Dialectic of Aesthetic Judgment, and hints at a new argument. The demand could be legitimate, he suggests, because there is a close connection between beauty and morality. Thus, it is possible that the deduction is not actually complete until much later in the third *Critique* than we are initially led to believe.

In fact, it is not until Section 59 of the Dialectic that Kant gestures toward an argument that some commentators take to be the true completion of the deduction. There, he writes:

> Now, I say, the beautiful is the symbol of the morally good, and only in this light (a point of view natural to every one, and one which every one exacts from others as a duty) does it give us pleasure with an attendant claim to the agreement of every one else, whereupon the mind becomes conscious of a certain ennoblement and elevation above mere sensibility to pleasure from impressions of sense, and also appraises the worth of others on the score of a like maxim of their judgement.[27]

Kant is claiming, in the first place, that the beautiful is the "symbol" of the morally good. On his view, for one thing to be a symbol of another thing, the first must be analogous with the second in relevant ways. For example, a monarchical state may be symbolized in various ways, including as "a living body when it is governed by constitutional laws" and "as a mere machine (like a hand-mill) when it is governed by an individual absolute will."[28] Kant maintains that while, strictly speaking, there is no "likeness" between a despotic state and a hand-mill, there is a likeness "between the rules of reflection upon both and their causality."[29]

There are, of course, further details to Kant's theory of symbolism;[30] but, what is clear even without entering into these details is that, if the beautiful is the symbol of the morally good, then there will need to be a sense in which beauty and morality are relevantly analogous. And Kant holds that there are at least four analogies between them. One analogy is that, in both cases, we find the manifestation of both freedom and harmony. In the case of a judgment of beauty, these are said to be features of our cognitive faculties: "the freedom of the imagination (consequently of our faculty in respect of its sensibility) is, in estimating the beautiful, represented as in accord with the understanding's conformity to law;" and in the case of a moral judgment, Kant maintains, "the freedom of the will is thought as the harmony of the latter with itself according to universal laws of Reason." Next, Kant maintains that there is an analogy when it comes to the universal character of judgments of beauty and morality. In the case of beauty, Kant claims, "[t]he subjective principle of the estimate of the beautiful is represented as *universal*, i.e. valid for every man" and, in the case of morality, the "objective principle of morality is set forth as also universal, i.e. for all individuals, and, at the same time, for all actions of the same individual." The remaining two analogies that Kant finds between beauty and morality have primarily to do with the similar nature of the pleasures connected with each. Thus, Kant claims that both the experience of beauty and of moral action please immediately, rather than instrumentally, and that both please "apart from all interest."[31]

Kant's underlying point is that, given that beauty and morality are relevantly analogous, it ought to be possible to use a sensible intuition of beauty to represent symbolically the non-sensible (because purely rational) idea of the morally good. For subjects who grasp this symbolism, judgments of beauty will perhaps provide a means to reflect on the morally good itself – and this is perhaps somehow relevant to the justification of demanding that others share our pleasure in what we find to be beautiful. The trouble is that, even if there is a sense in which the beautiful is the symbol of the morally good, Kant's explanation as to what this might have to do with the justification of aesthetic demands is so cursory that it is difficult to know precisely what it is supposed to be. One interpretive strategy has been to take Kant's argument to be that, as part of a judgment of taste, we make a *moral* demand that others be sensitive to and take an interest in that which symbolizes morality, or that which is morality's "supersensible" basis; and since beauty symbolizes morality, we have the right to demand that others be sensitive to and take an interest in beauty. This is why we are entitled to demand that others share in our aesthetic appraisals.[32] Such an argument clearly depends on a number of controversial premises, and its success is far from guaranteed at the outset.

As is clear, it is by no means obvious that Kant's deduction succeeds on its own terms. This is not to mention that it potentially faces a fundamental difficulty which has to do with the very motivation behind Kant's project of attempting to legitimate claims of taste. Many readers will be quite surprised by the analysis of the logical form of aesthetic judgments that in Kant's view gives rise to the need for a deduction. Specifically, it is apparently part of the underlying logical form of judgments of taste that they manifest universality and make demands upon others. But it is not obvious that we would grossly misunderstand the words "beautiful" and "sublime" if we thought that they can be properly applied purely subjectively, so that we can find something to be beautiful or sublime without demanding others' concurrence or blaming them for disagreeing. If a judgment of taste is not, in the end, one in which we have such expectations and make such demands, then the entire issue of the deduction becomes more or less academic. It will be a solution to a merely hypothetical problem rather than one that we actually face.

Now, Kant could simply insist that using the words "beauty" and "sublimity" in these subjective ways does, in fact, betray a serious misunderstanding of these words. He could perhaps suggest that those who insist on such ways of speaking likely do so because they have never actually experienced beauty or sublimity, but only mistakenly believe that they have; they perhaps call beautiful what they ought only to call "agreeable." The obvious difficulty with such a strategy, however, is that the dispute between Kant and these opponents would be near impossible to resolve. Each party could claim better to understand the meaning of "beauty" and "sublimity," and insist on sticking to his or her own account of the conditions of the use of these words (and the linguistic evidence itself could, in the end, favor Kant's opponents on this matter).

It is clear that whatever difficulties it faces insofar as it offers an account of the validity of judgments of taste, Kant's deduction of taste remains of substantial philosophical interest, and engaging with this aspect of his aesthetic theory is a worthwhile endeavor. Of course, doing this has not been our aim. And this brings us back to the issue at hand. Assuming that we had reason to prefer wholly *a priori* investigations in philosophical aesthetics over those grounded partly in empirical claims, might we have reason to think that we find such an investigation in the side of Kant's aesthetics that is taken up with the issue of justification? If so, might we not be right to suppose that Kant's true intention is to present us with an aesthetic theory that is wholly *a priori*?

Although it is obvious that Kant is concerned to take on empiricist opponents both in developing his aesthetic theory and elsewhere, it does not follow from this that the methods he employs in doing so import nothing empirical. We see quite clearly that Kant takes on Burke's empiricism in the General Remark at the end of Section 29 of the third

Critique. Kant here provides in rapid succession several distinct but related transcendental arguments that aim at attacking Burke. We have seen that Burke seeks to explain the experience of beauty in purely physiological terms. As Kant puts it, Burke maintains that the experience of beauty consists in "the relaxing, slackening, and enervating of the fibres of the body, and consequently a softening, a dissolving, a languor, and a fainting, dying, and melting away for pleasure."[33] Kant argues that this kind of explanation falls short of explaining what he takes to be the justified claim to universality of judgments of beauty: "if we attribute the delight in the object wholly and entirely to the gratification which it affords through charm or emotion, then we must not exact from *any one else* agreement with the aesthetic judgement passed by *us*."[34]

Kant does not state the anti-empiricist arguments of Section 29 as fully as we might hope, and so they would require some reconstruction in order fully to be assessed. But simply for the purpose of illustrating the point at issue, here, in outline, is one example. First, Kant claims, "[empirical] laws yield only a knowledge of how we do judge, but they do not give us a command as to how we ought to judge."[35] However, judgments of taste presuppose such commands. Therefore, such judgments, if valid, must not be founded on empirical laws – but must rather be founded upon an *a priori* principle. We see even in this brief statement that we are dealing with an argument that is in some sense anti-empiricist. Burke apparently believes that he can fully explain the given phenomenon simply by invoking empirical laws, such as laws concerning events that typically occur in the human body during experiences of beauty. But he has failed to recognize, according to Kant, that if an account of beauty is grounded merely on such empirical observations, then it will be unable to explain how it is that we are justified in demanding that others share in our pleasure. The reason why this is an anti-empiricist argument, then, is because it has the aim of defending the claim that judgments of taste must be grounded in an *a priori* principle. Such an *a priori* principle "lifts them out of the sphere of empirical psychology, in which otherwise they would remain buried amid the feelings of gratification and pain" and serves to "introduce them into transcendental philosophy."[36]

Although Kant is against empiricist accounts of *aesthetic judgments* such as Burke's, this does not mean that Kant's *aesthetic theory* rests on theses that are wholly *a priori*. In fact, the account that we are ultimately given appears to depend on what is, on the surface at any rate, the empirical thesis that the pleasure underlying judgments of taste is correlated with a certain kind of mental activity, namely the "harmony of the faculties." This is not to rule out that there could be interpretations of the side of Kant's aesthetics that emphasizes the issue of justification on which it is plausibly viewed as a theory arrived at through the application of wholly *a priori* methods. It is merely to suggest that such an interpretation is by no means obvious. And this, in turn, should give us reason to be open to the aspect of Kantian aesthetics that we have been pursuing here, which unashamedly rests on empirical elements of Kant's account of culture.

Notes

1   See Henry Allison, *Kant's Theory of Taste: A Reading of the Critique of Aesthetic Judgment* (Cambridge: Cambridge University Press), 2001, 54.

2   For an interpretation along these lines, see David Shier, "Why Kant Finds Nothing Ugly," *British Journal of Aesthetics* 38, no. 4 (1998): 412–418.

3   FI 20:224.

4   CJ 5:238. Cf. Magnitudes 2:182; Metaphysics 29:1010.

5   CJ 5:445.

6   Morals 6:456. Actually, ingratitude may not always be the most appropriate term to describe this individual's emotional state, at least on Kant's understanding of the term. For gratitude and ingratitude are responses to a benefactor who is perceived as having acted out of love toward us (Morals 6:455). But, at least in some cases, there may be a question as to whether we can be expected to perceive the maker (real or hypothetical) of an ugly object as having acted out of love to begin with. Perhaps the experience of ugliness in nature is one in which our first response is to attribute to a hypothetical maker an action that had nothing to do with love (whether or not such a response is warranted). Still, it remains possible for a maker to have created something we experience as ugly even while having done his or her best to make something we would experience as beautiful, and to have done so out of love.

7   Morals 6:459.

8   Morals 6:402.

9   Morals 6:402.

10   Anthropology 7:119.

11   Anthropology 7:120.

12   Anthropology 7:121.

13   David Hume, "Of the Standard of Taste," in *Essays, Moral, Political, and Literary* (Indianapolis: Liberty Classics, 1987), 231–258.

14   It should be noted that some commentators locate a "first attempt" at a deduction occurring in the Fourth Moment of the Analytic of the Beautiful, in Section 21. See for example Paul Guyer, *Kant and the Claims of Taste* (Cambridge: Cambridge University Press), ch. 8; see also Karl Ameriks, "How to Save Kant's Deduction of Taste," *Journal of Value Inquiry* 16, no. 4 (1982): 295–302.

15   CJ 5:279.

16   CJ 5:212.

17   CJ 5:212–213.

18   CJ 5:288.

19   CJ 5:289–290.

20   CJ 5:290f.

21   CJ 5:292–293. However, there is not a consensus among commentators when it comes to articulating the relevant *a priori* principle of taste. Luigi Caranti, for example, adopts an interpretation that is similar to the one suggested here, and maintains that the principle in question is bound up with the fact that our cognitive faculties are capable of a harmonious interaction; see "Logical Purposiveness and the Principle of Taste," *Kant-Studien* 96, no. 3 (2005): 364–374. On the other hand, Hannah Ginsborg maintains that the principle of taste is identical with the principle underlying the capacity for reflective judgment, more generally – namely, the principle of the systematicity of nature; see "Reflective Judgment and Taste," *Noûs* 24, no. 1 (1990): 76.

22   See Theodore Gracyk, "Sublimity, Ugliness, and Formlessness in Kant's Aesthetic Theory," *Journal of Aesthetics and Art Criticism* 45, no. 1 (1986): 49–56. Cf. Shier, "Why Kant Finds Nothing Ugly."

23   For such a view, see Allison, *Kant's Theory of Taste*, 186; Kant himself mentions the notion of proportionate accord at CJ 5:219. Similarly Ameriks, "How to Save Kant's Deduction of Taste," 299–300, claims that Kant holds that beautiful objects are those that give rise to harmonious experiences.

24   Allison's view is that it is appropriate to attribute to Kant's deduction a modest aim that does not include establishing that we are justified in particular cases, and that judged by this standard, the deduction is a success (*Kant's Theory of Taste*, 177). By contrast, Guyer claims that the deduction's failing to establish justification in particular cases is a substantial problem for Kant (*Kant and the Claims of Taste*, 242).

25   CJ 5:290f.

26   CJ 5:296.

27 CJ 5:353.
28 CJ 5:352.
29 CJ 5:352.
30 For a general exploration of Kant's views on symbolic representation, see Heiner Bielefeldt, *Symbolic Representation in Kant's Practical Philosophy* (Cambridge: Cambridge University Press, 2003).
31 CJ 5:354.
32 Donald Crawford pursues this aspect of Kant's account in some detail in *Kant's Aesthetic Theory* (Madison: University of Wisconsin Press, 1989), 157–159. R. K. Elliott also pursues a moral reconstruction of the argument of the deduction in "The Unity of Kant's 'Critique of Aesthetic Judgement,'" *British Journal of Aesthetics* 8, no. 3 (1968): 244–259. We find opposition to the view that the argument of the deduction rests on an appeal to morality in Guyer, *Kant and the Claims of Taste*, ch. 11; Allison, *Kant's Theory of Taste*, 180; and Claude MacMillan, "Kant's Deduction of Pure Aesthetic Judgments," *Kant-Studien* 76, no. 1–4 (1985): 43–54. John Zammito addresses connections between the symbolism in question and the idea that there is a supersensible aspect of subjectivity in *The Genesis of Kant's Critique of Judgment* (Chicago: University of Chicago Press, 1992), 275.
33 CJ 5:277–278.
34 CJ 5:277–278.
35 CJ 5:278.
36 CJ 5:266.

Bibliography

Allison, Henry. *Kant's Theory of Freedom.* Cambridge: Cambridge University Press, 1990.

Allison, Henry. *Kant's Theory of Taste: A Reading of the Critique of Aesthetic Judgment.* Cambridge: Cambridge University Press, 2001.

Allison, Henry. "Teleology and History in Kant: The Critical Foundations of Kant's Philosophy of History." In *Kant's Idea for a Universal History with a Cosmopolitan Aim*, edited by Amélie Oksenberg Rorty and James Schmidt, 24–45. Cambridge: Cambridge University Press, 2009.

Ameriks, Karl. "How to Save Kant's Deduction of Taste." *Journal of Value Inquiry* 16, no. 4 (1982): 295–302.

Ameriks, Karl. "Kant's Deduction of Freedom and Morality." *Journal of the History of Philosophy* 19, no. 1 (2008): 53–79.

Anderson, Elizabeth. "Emotions in Kant's Later Moral Philosophy: Honour and the Phenomenology of Moral Value." In *Kant's Ethics of Virtue*, edited by Monika Betzler. Berlin: Walter de Gruyter, 2008.

Beck, Lewis White. "Did the Sage of Königsberg Have No Dreams?" In *Essays on Kant and Hume.* New Haven: Yale University Press, 1978.

Beiser, Frederick C. *Diotima's Children.* Oxford: Oxford University Press, 2009.

Bielefeldt, Heiner. *Symbolic Representation in Kant's Practical Philosophy.* Cambridge: Cambridge University Press, 2003.

The Possibility of Culture: Pleasure and Moral Development in Kant's Aesthetics,
First Edition. Bradley Murray.
© 2015 John Wiley & Sons, Inc. Published 2015 by John Wiley & Sons, Inc.

Bruford, W. H. *The German Tradition of Self-Cultivation: "Bildung" from Humboldt to Thomas Mann*. Cambridge: Cambridge University Press, 2010.

Budd, Malcolm. "Delight in the Natural World: Kant on the Aesthetic Appreciation of Nature. Part III: The Sublime in Nature." *British Journal of Aesthetics* 38, no. 3 (1998): 233–250.

Burke, Edmund. *A Philosophical Enquiry into the Origin of Our Ideas of the Sublime and Beautiful*. Oxford: Oxford University Press, 2008.

Caranti, Luigi. "Logical Purposiveness and the Principle of Taste." *Kant-Studien* 96, no. 3 (2005): 364–374.

Carroll, Noel. "Art and Ethical Criticism: An Overview of Recent Directions of Research." *Ethics* 110, no. 2 (January 2000): 350–387.

Chignell, Andrew. "Kant's Concepts of Justification." *Noûs* 41, no. 1 (2007): 33–63.

Clewis, Robert. *The Kantian Sublime and the Revelation of Freedom*. Cambridge: Cambridge University Press, 2009.

Cocalis, Susan L. "The Transformation of 'Bildung' From an Image to an Ideal." *Monatshefte* 70, no. 4 (1978): 399–414.

Crawford, Donald. *Kant's Aesthetic Theory*. Madison: University of Wisconsin Press, 1974.

Crowther, Paul. *The Kantian Sublime: From Morality to Art*. Oxford: Oxford University Press, 1989.

Danto, Arthur C. *The Abuse of Beauty: Aesthetics and the Concept of Art*. Chicago: Open Court, 2003.

Darwall, Stephen. "Kant on Respect, Dignity, and the Duty of Respect." In *Kant's Ethics of Virtue*, edited by Monika Betzler, 175–200. Berlin: Walter de Gruyter, 2008.

Dickie, George. "The Myth of the Aesthetic Attitude." *American Philosophical Quarterly* 1, no. 1 (1964): 56–65.

Duchamp, Marcel. *The Late Show*. By Joan Bakewell. BBC, June 15, 1968.

Elliott, R. K. "The Unity of Kant's 'Critique of Aesthetic Judgement.'" *British Journal of Aesthetics* 8, no. 3 (1968): 244–259.

Eze, Emmanuel Chukwudi. "The Color of Reason: The Idea of 'Race' in Kant's Anthropology." In *Postcolonial African Philosophy: A Reader*, edited by Emmanuel Chukwudi Eze, 103–140. Oxford: Blackwell, 1997.

Gadamer, Hans-Georg. *Truth and Method*. London: Continuum, 2004.

Gasché, Rodolphe. *The Idea of Form: Rethinking Kant's Aesthetics*. Stanford: Stanford University Press, 2003.

Gaut, Berys. *Art, Emotion and Ethics*. Oxford: Oxford University Press, 2009.

Ginsborg, Hannah. "Reflective Judgment and Taste." *Noûs* 24, no. 1 (1990): 63–78.

Gracyk, Theodore. "Sublimity, Ugliness, and Formlessness in Kant's Aesthetic Theory." *Journal of Aesthetics and Art Criticism* 45, no. 1 (1986): 49–56.

Guyer, Paul. "Interest, Nature, and Art: A Problem in Kant's Aesthetics." *Review of Metaphysics* 31, no. 4 (1978): 580–603.

Guyer, Paul. "Pleasure and Society in Kant's Theory of Taste." In *Essays in Kant's Aesthetics*, edited by Paul Guyer and Ted Cohen, 87–114. Chicago: University of Chicago Press, 1982.

Guyer, Paul. *Kant and the Experience of Freedom.* Cambridge: Cambridge University Press, 1996.

Guyer, Paul. *Kant and the Claims of Taste.* Cambridge: Cambridge University Press, 1997.

Guyer, Paul. *Kant's System of Nature and Freedom: Selected Essays.* Oxford: Clarendon Press, 2005.

Guyer, Paul. *Values of Beauty.* Cambridge: Cambridge University Press, 2005.

Hickey, Dave. *The Invisible Dragon: Four Essays on Beauty.* Los Angeles: Art Issues Press/Foundation for Advanced Critical Studies, 1993.

Horn, Christoph. "The Concept of Love in Kant's Virtue Ethics." In *Kant's Ethics of Virtue*, edited by Monika Betzler, 147–174. Berlin: Walter de Gruyter, 2008.

Hume, David. "Of the Standard of Taste." In *Essays, Moral, Political, and Literary*, 231–258. Indianapolis: Liberty Classics, 1987.

Hutcheson, Francis. *An Inquiry into the Original of Our Ideas of Beauty and Virtue in Two Treatises.* Indianapolis: Liberty Fund, 2008.

Kemp, Gary. "The Aesthetic Attitude." *British Journal of Aesthetics* 39, no. 4 (1999): 392–399.

Kivy, Peter. *The Possessor and the Possessed: Handel, Mozart, Beethoven, and the Idea of Musical Genius.* New Haven: Yale University Press, 2001.

Kleingeld, Pauline. "Kant's Second Thoughts on Race." *The Philosophical Quarterly* 57, no. 229 (2007): 573–592.

Leibniz, Gottfried Wilhelm. *Philosophical Papers and Letters: A Selection.* Edited by Leroy E. Loemker. Dordrecht: Springer, 1989.

Levinson, Jerrold. *Aesthetics and Ethics.* Cambridge: Cambridge University Press, 2001.

Lewis, Peter. "'Original Nonsense': Art and Genius in Kant's Aesthetic." In *Kant and His Influence*, edited by G. MacDonald Ross and T. McWalter, 126–145. Bristol: Thoemmes, 1990.

Lopes, Dominic McIver. *Beyond Art.* Oxford: Oxford University Press, 2014.

Lorand, Ruth. "Free and Dependent Beauty: A Puzzling Issue." *British Journal of Aesthetics* 29, no. 1 (1989): 32–40.

Louden, Robert B. *Kant's Impure Ethics: From Rational Beings to Human Beings.* Oxford: Oxford University Press, 2002.

MacMillan, Claude. "Kant's Deduction of Pure Aesthetic Judgments." *Kant-Studien* 76, no. 1–4 (1985): 43–54.

Marcuse, Herbert. *The Aesthetic Dimension*. Boston: Beacon Press, 1979.

McFarland, John. *Kant's Concept of Teleology*. Edinburgh: University of Edinburgh Press, 1970.

Mendelssohn, Moses. *Moses Mendelssohn: Philosophical Writings*. Edited by Daniel O. Dahlstrom. Cambridge: Cambridge University Press, 1997.

Morrisson, Iain. *Kant and the Role of Pleasure in Moral Action*. Athens: Ohio University Press, 2008.

Munzel, G. Felicitas. *Kant's Conception of Moral Character: The "Critical" Link of Morality, Anthropology, and Reflective Judgment*. Chicago: University of Chicago Press, 1999.

Murdoch, Iris. *The Sovereignty of Good*. London: Ark Paperbacks, Routledge & Kegan Paul, 1985.

Murray, Bradley. "Kant on Genius and Art." *The British Journal of Aesthetics* 47, no. 2 (2007): 199–214.

Nehamas, Alexander. *Only a Promise of Happiness: The Place of Beauty in a World of Art*. Princeton: Princeton University Press, 2010.

Pogge, Thomas. "Kant on Ends and the Meaning of Life." In *Reclaiming the History of Ethics: Essays for John Rawls*, edited by Andrews Reath, Barbara Herman, and Christine M. Korsgaard, 361–387. Cambridge: Cambridge University Press, 1997.

Rogerson, Kenneth F. *The Problem of Free Harmony in Kant's Aesthetics*. Albany: SUNY Press, 2008.

Rotenstreich, Nathan. "Morality and Culture: A Note on Kant." *History of Philosophy Quarterly* 6 (1989): 303–316.

Rousseau, Jean-Jacques. *Rousseau: "The Discourses" and Other Early Political Writings*. Edited by Victor Gourevitch. Cambridge: Cambridge University Press, 1997.

Schaper, Eva. "Taste, Sublimity, and Genius." In *The Cambridge Companion to Kant*, edited by P. Guyer, 367–393. Cambridge: Cambridge University Press, 1992.

Seigel, Jerrold E. *The Private Worlds of Marcel Duchamp*. Berkeley: University of California Press, 1995.

Shaftesbury, Anthony Ashley Cooper, Third Earl of. *Characteristics of Men, Manners, Opinions, Times*. Cambridge: Cambridge University Press, 1999.

Shier, David. "Why Kant Finds Nothing Ugly." *British Journal of Aesthetics* 38, no. 4 (1998): 412–418.

Steiner, Wendy. *Venus in Exile*. New York: The Free Press, 2001.

Stolnitz, Jerome. "On the Origins of 'Aesthetic Disinterestedness.'" *Journal of Aesthetics and Art Criticism* 20, no. 2 (1961): 131–143.

Stolnitz, Jerome. "'The Aesthetic Attitude' in the Rise of Modern Aesthetics." *The Journal of Aesthetics and Art Criticism* 36, no. 4 (1978): 409–422.

Stratton-Lake, Philip. "Being Virtuous and the Virtues: Two Aspects of Kant's Doctrine of Virtue." In *Kant's Ethics of Virtue*, edited by Monika Betzler, 101–122. Berlin: Walter de Gruyter, 2008.

Uehling, Theodore Edward. *The Notion of Form in Kant's Critique of Aesthetic Judgement*. The Hague: Mouton, 1971.

Wiggins, David. *Sameness and Substance Renewed*. Cambridge: Cambridge University Press, 2001.

Williams, Howard L. *Kant's Political Philosophy*. Oxford: Basil Blackwell, 1986.

Wolff, Christian. *Psychologia Empirica*. Edited by Jean École. Hildesheim: Georg Olms, 1968.

Wood, Allen. *Kant's Ethical Thought*. Cambridge: Cambridge University Press, 1999.

Wood, Allen. "Kant and the Problem of Human Nature." In *Essays on Kant's Anthropology*, edited by Brian Jacobs and Patrick Kain. Cambridge: Cambridge University Press, 2003.

Wood, Allen. "Kant's Fourth Proposition: The Unsociable Sociability of Human Nature." In *Kant's Idea for a Universal History with a Cosmopolitan Aim*, edited by Amélie Oksenberg Rorty and James Schmidt. Cambridge: Cambridge University Press, 2009.

Zammito, John H. *The Genesis of Kant's Critique of Judgment*. Chicago: University of Chicago Press, 1992.

Zangwill, Nick. "Unkantian Notions of Disinterest." *British Journal of Aesthetics* 32, no. 2 (1992): 149–152.

Zuckert, Rachel. *Kant on Beauty and Biology*. Cambridge: Cambridge University Press, 2007.

Index

a priori, 56, 125, 127–9, 133–5

abstraction, 8, 54, 73, 75, 77–80, 97

affect, 24, 93–6
   languid, 93
   strenuous, 93

anger, 93

animality, 19–21, 87

anthrophobia, 93

apathy, 24, 95–6

apprehension, 55–6, 90–91

art, 6, 66–9, 71, 75–80, 105, 110
   aesthetic, 79
   agreeable, 79
   fine, 67, 76, 78–80

artifact, 71–2, 98, 110–111

beneficence, 38, 113

Burke, Edmund, 17, 31–2, 48, 133–4

categorical imperative, 106–7

categories, 53

colonialism, 5

colossal, 96

contra-finality, 88–9, 91–3, 122

culture, 2, 4–5, 8–9, 13, 15, 17, 19–23, 25, 58, 66, 70, 105–7, 109, 111–14, 118, 125–6, 135

deduction of taste, 133

delirium, 94

desire, 16, 31–2, 46–9, 51–2, 54–5, 67, 70, 72–5, 78–80, 99, 124

desperation, 93, 99

Diogenes, 14

disappointment with humanity, 93–4

disinterestedness, 8, 46–7, 54, 57, 68, 70, 73, 124

Duchamp, Marcel, 79–80

duty, 16, 20, 22–26, 40–41, 58, 69, 106, 108–9, 130–131

empiricism, 131
end, 36, 50–51, 71–4, 77–9, 85, 96,
    106–13, 115–18
    ultimate end of nature, 105,
        109–11, 115–18
enthusiasm, 94–5
equality, 2–3, 94
evil, 16

fanaticism, 94
fantasy, 94
finality, 8, 32–5, 54, 73, 75, 77,
    79–80, 87–9, 91–3, 97,
    109–10, 115, 122, 129
    intrinsic, 109–10
    subjective, 8, 32–5, 54, 129
freedom, 2–5, 16, 41, 95, 131
function, 37, 51, 79–80, 111

genius, 8, 74–9
gratitude, 8, 33–9, 41, 124

handicraft, 78
happiness, 2, 9, 14, 38, 109,
    112–14, 118
harmony, 76, 106, 123,
    129–31, 135
hate, 124–5
humanity, 2, 19–21, 70, 86, 89,
    93–4, 106–11, 114–18
Hume, David, 6–7, 127

inclinations, 2–4, 14, 16–23, 26,
    32, 39–41, 46–7, 57–8, 84–8,
    92, 94–6, 99, 105, 109, 112,
    114, 124–5
infinite, 91
ingratitude, 94, 124–5

judgments of taste, 6–7, 123,
    127–8, 130, 133–5

Kant's works
    *An Answer to the Question: What is
        Enlightenment?*, 3
    *Anthropology from a Pragmatic
        Point of View*, 7, 15–16, 24, 58,
        68, 95, 125
    Critique of Judgment, 7, 18, 31,
        33–4, 36, 46–7, 52–3, 55,
        67–9, 73, 76, 84, 94–5, 109,
        115, 123, 127, 131
    Critique of Practical Reason, 39,
        85, 88
    Critique of Pure Reason, 53, 55,
        90, 115–16
    Essay on the Maladies of the Head,
        16, 94
    *First Introduction to the Critique
        of Judgment*, 123
    *Groundwork of the Metaphysics
        of Morals*, 9, 22, 106–7,
        109, 118
    *Idea for a Universal History with a
        Cosmopolitan Aim*, 3, 21, 70, 113
    Lectures on Anthropology, 4
    Lectures on Ethics, 14
    Lectures on Pedagogy, 16, 19, 57
    The Metaphysics of Morals, 5, 7, 9,
        16, 21, 23–4, 31, 39, 41, 46,
        52, 69, 85, 95, 106, 108–9,
        118, 125
    *Observations on the Beautiful and
        the Sublime*, 40, 85, 98
    *On the Common Saying: That May
        be True in Theory, But It is of No
        Use in Practice*, 2
    Toward Perpetual Peace, 5

labor, 51, 78
love, 3, 8–9, 17–18, 22–4, 31–2,
    38–41, 54, 58, 75, 84–5, 94,
    114, 124–5

pathological, 40–41, 85
  practical, 39–40
luxury, 13–15

magnitude, 89–91, 96
might, 87–88, 92–3
misanthropy, 93, 125
monstrous, 96
moral feeling, 18, 31, 39, 98 *see also*
  love, respect
moral law, 23, 85, 88, 107
moral principles, 25, 86, 96
moralization, 19, 21, 108, 118
Murdoch, Iris, 66, 80

passions, 16, 57, 67
pleasure, 1, 2, 4, 6–9, 13–19, 21–2,
  24–6, 32–9, 46–59, 66–70,
  72–3, 75–7, 79–80, 84–5,
  88–9, 95–6, 98–9, 105–9, 118,
  122–5, 127, 129–32, 134–5
  of agreeableness, 15–17, 33,
    35–7, 46–9, 52, 57, 99, 128
  of beauty, 1, 7–9, 17–18, 32–4,
    37–9, 46–50, 52, 54–8, 72, 75,
    79–80, 84, 89
  contemplative, 46, 53
  of goodness, 36–7, 49–52, 54,
    67–8, 75, 99, 111
  of perfection, 37, 50
  practical, 52
  of utility, 37–8
pragmatic anthropology, 9, 125–6
purpose, 20, 74, 110–12
purposiveness *see* finality

qualitative perfection, 36–7
quantitative perfection, 36–7

race, 4–5, 112–13
rationalists, 50

reason, 3, 19–21, 23, 25–6,
  35, 40, 50, 52, 71, 73, 77,
  86, 91, 96, 106, 109, 111,
  115–18, 131
  public use of, 3
  regulative use of, 35, 115–17
reflective judgment, 87, 115, 117
respect, 8, 18, 39–40, 84–6, 89, 108
  pathological, 85
  practical, 39, 85
revolution, 95
Rousseau, Jean-Jacques, 1–2, 7,
  13–15, 18, 48, 66–8, 80,
  105, 118

Shaftesbury, Earl of, 17
slavery, 5
sociability, 3–4
social progress, 2, 4, 15
subjectivity of taste, 6, 34, 127
sublimity, 2, 8–9, 18, 36, 84–9,
  91–4, 96–9, 105, 122–3,
  128–9, 133
  artistic, 96, 98
  dynamical, 89, 92–3, 98
  in internal nature, 93, 98
  mathematical, 89, 91–2, 96–8
subreption, 89, 93–6, 98
supersensible, 87, 132
sympathy, 22, 24–5, 40–41
synthesis, 53, 55–6, 89–90

teleology, 79
transcendental idealism, 87

ugliness, 9, 80, 122–5

virtue, 23–4, 40, 58, 68–70

Warhol, Andy, 79
will, 21, 51, 113